NorthStar

Focus on Reading and Writing

Intermediate

Laurie Betta

Carolyn DuPaquier Sardinas

SERIES EDITORS
Frances Boyd
Carol Numrich

NorthStar: Focus on Reading and Writing, Intermediate

Addison Wesley Longman, 10 Bank Street, White Plains, NY 10606

Senior acquisitions editor: Allen Ascher
Development editor: Debbie Sistino
Director of design and production: Rhea Banker
Production manager: Marie McNamara
Managing editor: Halley Gatenby
Production editor: Liza Pleva
Photo research: Diana Nott
Cover design: Rhea Banker
Cover illustration: Robert Delaunay's Circular Forms, Sun No. 2,
   1912–1913. Giraudon/Art Resource, NY. L&M SERVICES
   B.V., Amsterdam 970902
Text design and composition: Delgado Design, Inc.
Manufacturing supervisor: Edie Pullman

Photo credits: p.1, PEPSI, PEPSI·COLA, GENERATION NEXT and
   the Pepsi Globe design are trademarks of PepsiCo, Inc.; p. 67,
   cockroach, Animals Animals, © Raymond A. Mendez; p. 79,
   (a) monarch butterfly eggs, Animals Animals, © Breck P. Kent,
   (b) monarch larvae, Animals Animals, © Raymond A. Mendez,
   (c) monarch chrysalis, Animals Animals, © Breck P. Kent,
   (d) monarch butterfly, Animals Animals, © E.R. Degginger;
   p. 111, (left) Greg Louganis diving, AP/Wide World Photos, (right)
   AIDS demonstration, AP/Wide World Photos; p. 157, © 1996,
   Comstock, Inc.; p. 177, UPI/Corbis Bettman

Art credits: pp. 1, 14, 45, 98, 173, 192, 197, 209, Hal Just; p. 21,
   Dusan Petricic; p. 135, Andrew Singer; p. 144, June 28, 1996,
   Los Angeles Times

Library of Congress Cataloging-in-Publication Data

Sardinas, Carolyn DuPaquier
   NorthStar, Focus on Reading and Writing Intermediate/Carolyn
   DuPaquier Sardinas, Laurie Betta
      p.   cm.
   ISBN 0-201-69422-0 (pbk.)
    1. English Language—Textbooks for foreign speakers. 2. Reading
comprehension—Problems, exercises, etc. 3. Writing—Problems, exer-
cises etc. I. Betta, Laurie. II. Title.
PE1128.S593 1998   97-41536
428.3'4—dc21   CIP

2 3 4 5 6 7 8 9 10-RTN-02 01 00 99 98

CONTENTS

INTRODUCTION

NorthStar is an innovative four-level, integrated skills series for learners of English as a Second or Foreign Language. The series is divided into two strands: listening/speaking and reading/writing. There are four books in each strand, taking students from the Basic to the Advanced level. The two books at each level explore different aspects of the same contemporary themes, which allows for reinforcement of both vocabulary and grammatical structures. Each strand and each book can also function independently as a skills course built on high-interest thematic content.

NorthStar is designed to work alongside Addison Wesley Longman's *Focus on Grammar* series, and students are referred directly to *Focus on Grammar* for further practice and detailed grammatical explanations.

NorthStar is written for students with academic as well as personal language goals, for those who want to learn English while exploring enjoyable, intellectually challenging themes.

NORTHSTAR'S PURPOSE

The *NorthStar* series grows out of our experience as teachers and curriculum designers, current research in second-language acquisition and pedagogy, as well as our beliefs about language teaching. It is based on five principles.

Principle One: In language learning, making meaning is all-important. The more profoundly students are stimulated intellectually and emotionally by what goes on in class, the more language they will use and retain. One way that classroom teachers can engage students in making meaning is by organizing language study thematically.

We have tried to identify themes that are up-to-date, sophisticated, and varied in tone—some lighter, some more serious—on ideas and issues of wide concern. The forty themes in *NorthStar* provide stimulating topics for the readings and the listening selections, including why people like dangerous sports, the effect of food on mood, an Olympic swimmer's fight against AIDS, experimental punishments for juvenile offenders, people's relationships with their cars, philanthropy, emotional intelligence, privacy in the workplace, and the influence of arts education on brain development.

Each corresponding unit of the integrated skills books explores two distinct topics related to a single theme as the chart below illustrates.

Theme	Listening/Speaking Topic	Reading/Writing Topic
Insects	Offbeat professor fails at breeding pests, then reflects on experience	Extract adapted from Kafka's "The Metamorphosis"
Personality	Shyness, a personal and cultural view	Definition of, criteria for, success

Principle Two: Second-language learners, particularly adults, need and want to learn both the form and content of the language. To accomplish this, it is useful to integrate language skills with the study of grammar, vocabulary, and American culture.

In *NorthStar*, we have integrated the skills in two strands: listening/speaking and reading/writing. Further, each thematic unit integrates the study of a grammatical point with related vocabulary and cultural information. When skills are integrated, language use inside of the classroom more closely mimics language use outside of the classroom. This motivates students. At the same time, the focus can shift back and forth from what is said to how it is said to the relationship between the two. Students are apt to use more of their senses, more of themselves. What goes on in the classroom can also appeal to a greater variety of learning styles. Gradually, the integrated-skills approach narrows the gap between the ideas and feelings students want to express in speaking and writing and their present level of English proficiency.

The link between the listening/speaking and reading/writing strands is close enough to allow students to explore the themes and review grammar and reinforce vocabulary, yet it is distinct enough to sustain their interest. Also, language levels and grammar points in *NorthStar* are keyed to Addison Wesley Longman's *Focus on Grammar* series.

Principle Three: Both teachers and students need to be active learners. Teachers must encourage students to go beyond whatever level they have reached.

With this principle in mind, we have tried to make the exercises creative, active, and varied. Several activities call for considered opinion and critical thinking. Also, the exercises offer students many opportunities for individual reflection, pair- and small-group learning, as well as out-of-class assignments for review and research. An answer key is printed on perfo-

rated pages in the back of each book so the teacher or students can remove it. A teacher's manual, which accompanies each book, features ideas and tips for tailoring the material to individual groups of students, planning the lessons, managing the class, and assessing students' progress.

Principle Four: Feedback is essential for language learners and teachers. If students are to become better able to express themselves in English, they need a response to both what they are expressing and how they are expressing it.

NorthStar's exercises offer multiple opportunities for oral and written feedback from fellow students and from the teacher. A number of open-ended opinion and inference exercises invite students to share and discuss their answers. In Information Gap, Fieldwork, and Presentation activities, students must present and solicit information and opinions from their peers as well as members of their communities. Throughout these activities, teachers may offer feedback on the form and content of students' language, sometimes on the spot and sometimes via audio/video recordings or notes.

Principle Five: The quality of relationships among the students and between the students and teacher is important, particularly in a language class where students are asked to express themselves on issues and ideas.

The information and activities in *NorthStar* promote genuine interaction, acceptance of differences, and authentic communication. By building skills and exploring ideas, the exercises help students participate in discussions and write essays of an increasingly more complex and sophisticated nature.

DESIGN OF THE UNITS

For clarity and ease of use, the listening/speaking and reading/writing strands follow the same unit outline given below. Each unit contains from 5 to 8 hours of classroom material. Teachers can customize the units by assigning some exercises for homework and/or skipping others. Exercises in sections 1–4 are essential for comprehension of the topic, while teachers may want to select among the activities in sections 5–7.

1. **Approaching the Topic**
A warm-up, these activities introduce students to the general context for listening or reading and get them personally connected to the topic. Typically, students might react to a visual image, describe a personal experience, or give an opinion orally or in writing.

2. **Preparing to Listen/Preparing to Read**
In this section, students are introduced to information and language to help them comprehend the specific tape or text they will study. They might read and react to a paragraph framing the topic, prioritize factors, or take a general-knowledge quiz and share information. In the vocabulary section, students work with words and expressions selected to help them with comprehension.

3. **Listening One/Reading One**
This sequence of four exercises guides students to listen or read with understanding and enjoyment by practicing the skills of (a) prediction, (b) comprehension of main ideas, (c) comprehension of details, and (d) inference. In activities of increasing detail and complexity, students learn to grasp and interpret meaning. The sequence culminates in an inference exercise that gets students to listen and read between the lines.

4. **Listening Two/Reading Two**
Here students work with a tape or text that builds on ideas from the first listening/reading. This second tape or text contrasts with the first in viewpoint, genre, and/or tone.

Activities ask students to explicitly relate the two pieces, consider consequences, distinguish and express points of view. In these exercises, students can attain a deeper understanding of the topic.

5. **Reviewing Language**
These exercises help students explore, review, and play with language from both of the selections. Using the thematic context, students focus on language: pronunciation, word forms, prefixes and suffixes, word domains, idiomatic expressions, analogies. The listening/speaking strand stresses oral exercises, while the reading/writing strand focuses on written responses.

6. **Skills for Expression**
Here students practice related grammar points across the theme in both topics. The grammar is practiced orally in the listening/speaking strand, and in writing in the reading/writing strand. For additional practice, teachers can turn to Addison Wesley Longman's *Focus on Grammar*, to which *NorthStar* is keyed by level and grammar points. In the Style section, students practice functions (listening/speaking) or rhetorical styles (reading/writing) that prepare them to express ideas on a higher level. Within each unit, students are led from controlled to freer practice of productive skills.

7. **On Your Own**
These activities ask students to apply the content, language, grammar, and style they have practiced in the unit. The exercises elicit a higher level of speaking or writing than students were capable of at the start of the unit. Speaking topics include role plays, surveys, presentations and experiments. Writing topics include paragraphs, letters, summaries, and academic essays.

In Fieldwork, the second part of On Your Own, students go outside of the classroom, using their knowledge and skills to gather data from personal interviews, library research, and telephone or Internet research. They report and reflect on the data in oral or written presentations to the class.

AN INVITATION

We think of a good textbook as a musical score or a movie script: It tells you the moves and roughly how quickly and in what sequence to make them. But until you and your students bring it to life, a book is silent and static, a mere possibility. We hope that *NorthStar* orients, guides, and interests you as teachers.

It is our hope that the *NorthStar* series stimulates your students' thinking, which in turn stimulates their language learning, and that they will have many opportunities to reflect on the viewpoints of journalists, commentators, researchers, other students, and people in the community. Further, we hope that *NorthStar* guides them to develop their own viewpoint on the many and varied themes encompassed by this series.

We welcome your comments and questions. Please send them to us at the publisher:

Frances Boyd and Carol Numrich, Editors
NorthStar
Addison Wesley Longman
10 Bank Street
White Plains, NY 10606-1951
or, by e-mail at:
awlelt@awl.com

ACKNOWLEDGMENTS

We would like to express our deep appreciation to Carol Numrich, Debbie Sistino, Allen Ascher, Luis Sardinas, Pete Dupaquier, Carolyn Reno, and our other colleagues at the American Language Program at California State University, Fullerton.

Laurie Betta
Carolyn DuPaquier Sardinas

THE WORLD OF ADVERTISING

APPROACHING THE TOPIC

A. PREDICTING

1 Look at the advertisement and discuss these questions.

1. What kind of people do you think are most likely to buy this product: teenagers, parents with young children, or senior citizens (age sixty-five and older)?

2. Is this kind of product popular in your home country? Is this kind of product advertised on television or on billboards?

2 Imagine that you are writing an advertisement for this product. Which three words from this list best describe the product: delicious, refreshing, powerful, expensive, cool?

1

B. SHARING INFORMATION

1 *Work in groups of four. Complete the chart with the names of products that you usually buy.*

PRODUCT	STUDENT 1	STUDENT 2	STUDENT 3	STUDENT 4
Drinks				
Shampoo				
Snack Food				
Toothpaste				

2 *Discuss the questions with your group.*

1. How often do you buy these products?

2. Do you know any TV commercials or other advertisements for these products? Can you describe the advertisements?

3. Do advertisements sometimes convince you to buy products?

PREPARING TO READ

A. BACKGROUND

How much do you know about the world of advertising? Test your knowledge. Read each statement and decide if it is true or false. Write T or F.

_____ **1.** To sell a product in a foreign country, a company must translate its advertisement.

_____ **2.** International businesses such as McDonald's offer different products in different parts of the world.

_____ **3.** When advertisers write an ad, their goal is to make people laugh.

_____ **4.** Laws about advertising are basically the same all over the world.

B. VOCABULARY FOR COMPREHENSION

Read the definitions. Then read the paragraph on page 4 that describes an imaginary new product. Fill in each blank with the correct form of one of the vocabulary words.

a campaign: a planned, organized effort

competition: 1. activity in which people are trying to do better than each other; 2. (then) people or things that you compete against

to convince: to make someone want to do something

to fail: to not do well, to not reach your goal

a firm: a company

global: international

a goal: something that people want to do

a market (to market): a group of people to whom products are sold (to try to sell a product to a certain group of people)

a message: information that one person gives to another

to succeed: to do well, to reach your goal

Many people are interested in getting more exercise. Some of them are able to (**1**) _____ in making exercise a regular part of their lives. Other people are never able to exercise regularly. They want to, but they (**2**) _____ to do so because their lives are very busy. People who exercise often buy bottled water. People who are interested in their health are also part of the (**3**) _____ for this product. Energy Plus is a group of scientists, sports players, and business people. The members of this (**4**) _____ are working together to make a new kind of bottled water for people who exercise regularly. The people at Energy Plus hope to make a product that will have a delicious taste. Their (**5**) _____ is to finish making this product in one year. Energy Plus bottled water will be advertised on television and in magazines. All the ads in this (**6**) _____ will begin on the same date, and they will all be similar. The (**7**) _message_ of the ads will be that drinking plenty of water is very important for people who exercise. A large number of people, both men and women, will be interested in the drink. The interest in this product will be (**8**) _____ . Energy Plus will provide a special telephone number to store owners. They can call this number to get information that will (**9**) _____ them to sell Energy Plus in their stores. Several other groups are working to make a similar product. Because of this (**10**) _____ , the people at Energy Plus must try to make the best product possible.

3 READING ONE: Advertising All Over the World

A. INTRODUCING THE TOPIC

Work with a partner. Discuss problems that you think advertisers might have if they want to sell a product in different countries. List two or three problems in the space below. Share your list with the class.

Possible Problems

_____

_____

_____

Now read the following magazine article on the subject of global advertising. How many of the problems that your class discussed are found in the article?

Larger than ever; more important oth any time before

Advertising All Over the World

1   How can a rabbit be stronger than a football hero? How can a rabbit be more powerful than a big, strong man? In the world of advertising, this is quite possible. Consider the example of Jacko. This great Australian football hero recently appeared on TV and yelled at the audience to buy products. Jacko's angry campaign worked well in Australia, so Energizer batteries invited him north to sell their product in the United States. But Jacko's yelling did not convince the American audience to buy batteries. So, good-bye, Jacko. Hello, Energizer Bunny, the little toy rabbit that has sold far more batteries than Jacko.

2   In the world of advertising, selling products is the most important goal. As companies are becoming more global, they are looking for new ways to sell their products all over the world. It is true that because of global communication, the world is becoming smaller today.

3   But it is also true that the problems of global advertising—problems of language and culture—have become larger than ever. For example, Braniff Airlines wanted to advertise its fine leather seats. But when its advertisement was translated from English to Spanish, it told people that they could fly naked! Another example of wrong translation is when Chevrolet tried to market the Chevy Nova in Latin America. In English, the word *nova* refers to a star. But in Spanish, it means "doesn't go." Would you buy a car with this name?

4   To avoid these problems of translation, most advertising firms are now beginning to write completely new ads. In writing new ads, global advertisers must consider different styles of communication in different countries. In some cultures, the meaning of an advertisement is usually found in the exact words that are used to describe the product and to explain why it is better than the competition. This is true in such countries as the United States, Britain, and Germany. But in other cultures, such as Japan's, the message depends more on situations and feelings than it does on words. For this reason, the goal of many TV commercials in Japan will be to show how good people feel in a party or some other social situation. The commercial will not say that a product is better than others. Instead, its goal will be to create a positive mood or feeling about the product.

5   Global advertisers must also consider differences in laws and customs. For instance, certain countries will not allow TV commercials on Sunday, and others will not allow TV commercials for children's products on any day of the week. In some

parts of the world, it is forbidden to show dogs on television or certain types of clothing, such as jeans. The global advertiser who does not understand such laws and customs will soon have problems.

6   Finally, there is the question of what to advertise. People around the world have different customs as well as different likes and dislikes. So the best advertisement in the world means nothing if the product is not right for the market. Even though some markets around the world are quite similar, companies such as McDonald's have found that it is very important to sell different products in different parts of the world. So when you go to a McDonald's in Hawaii,

you'll find Chinese noodles on the menu. If you stop for a hamburger in Germany, you can order a beer with your meal. In Malaysia, you can try a milk shake that is flavored with a fruit that most people in other countries have never tasted.

7   All of these products must be sold with the right kind of message. It has never been an easy job for global advertisers to create this message. But no matter how difficult this job may be, it is very important for global advertisers to do it well. In today's competitive world, most new products quickly fail. Knowing how to advertise in the global market can help companies win the competition for success.

B. READING FOR MAIN IDEAS

1 *Look at the true/false statements that you completed in Section 2A. Decide whether or not to change them according to information that you learned from Reading One. If a statement is false, rewrite it to make it true.*

Example: To sell a product in a foreign country, a company must ~~translate its~~ advertisement.
write a new

2 *Write short answers to the following questions. Then compare your answers with the class.*

1. Who is Jacko? What does he show about international advertising?

_____

2. What problem do advertisers have when they try to translate ads directly from one language to another?

_____

3. What must a global advertiser understand in order to avoid having problems?

_____

4. Why should a company offer different products in different countries?

_____

C. READING FOR DETAILS

Complete the sentences below with the most appropriate word.
Make sure that the sentences are correct according to the information
that you have read.

1. A battery _____ changed its campaign from Jacko to the Energizer Bunny.
   a. firm   c. market
   b. goal   d. translator

2. There are many problems with _____ , even with languages that are similar, such as English and Spanish.
   a. advertising   c. translation
   b. marketing   d. competition

3. Different countries have different styles of _____ , which involve different uses of words and feelings.
   a. writing   c. advertising
   b. communicating d. competing

4. Some countries do not allow _____ ads for children's products.
   a. newspaper   c. magazine
   b. TV   d. radio

5. Drinking beer with a meal is an example of a _____ .
   a. culture   c. custom
   b. style   d. law

6. Many new products fail because there is a lot of _____ in the world today.
   a. advertising   c. communication
   b. business   d. competition

7. The Nova campaign failed in Latin America because of the _____ of the ads.
   a. goal   c. style
   b. cost   d. message

8. Ads that show a group of people sharing good feelings are often quite successful in _____ .
   a. Germany   c. Malaysia
   b. Japan   d. Britain

D. READING BETWEEN THE LINES

Read the following plans for marketing and advertising campaigns. Do you think that these campaigns will be successful? Use information from Reading One to explain your opinion.

1. Frutico is a fruit drink company. Last year it had a pineapple juice product that was very successful in Mexico. This year it plans to sell the same product in Canada. This drink will be the first Frutico product sold in Canada.

Do you think the campaign will be successful?   Yes   No   Maybe

Explanation: _____

_____

_____

2. Jolie is a clothing firm that sells business suits for women. Last year it was not very successful. In order to save money, the firm has decided to pay a translator to translate its ads from French to Japanese. This costs less than paying a writer to create new ads.

Do you think the campaign will be successful?   Yes   No   Maybe

Explanation: _____

_____

_____

3. Happy Time is a company that sells children's toys. It plans to advertise its products on TV in several Asian countries. By using only one type of advertisement, it can save time and money. The competition does not advertise on television at all.

Do you think the campaign will be successful?   Yes   No   Maybe

Explanation: _____

_____

_____

4. Sandwich Express is a restaurant that will soon open new stores in Saudi Arabia. Each store will have several large signs advertising the use of Arabian spices in Sandwich Express products. These spices are not used in the home country of Sandwich Express.

Do you think the campaign will be successful?   Yes   No   Maybe

Explanation: _____

_____

_____

4 READING TWO: Changing World Markets

A. EXPANDING THE TOPIC

Read the following speech given by Julia Ross, the president of the Global Advertisers' Association. She recently spoke at a meeting of advertisers who want to start global campaigns. Part of her speech was published in Adworld *magazine. Consider the following questions and discuss them with the class before you read.*

1. Can you think of any countries in which the government might not allow businesses to advertise?

2. Are there any food products in your home country that might not sell well in other parts of the world? Where? Why?

3. Do you know anyone who has lived in a country where it is difficult for people to buy the products they want?

Changing World Markets

Adworld

1   Good morning. It's good to be here with you at this meeting. My goal is to give you some information about changing world markets. Let's start by looking at the U.S.A.—which we could say is the "United States of Advertising." Can you think of a country with more advertising than the U.S.? For example, you're watching a movie on TV. You're waiting for the good guy to get the bad guy, and BAM! There's a commercial. A few minutes later the good guy's in trouble, and BOOM! Another commercial. Message after message. It's not like that in other countries, folks. In places like France and Spain, you'll watch at least a half hour of the program, then you'll get some commercials. All in a row.

2   But I'm not here today to talk about Europe. Let's talk about China, where for years any kind of commercial advertising was illegal. Government advertising, yes— that was all over the place. But business advertising? No way! Then Sony came along and changed things. The Japanese companies were the first to start advertising in China. They've led the way for others to come into the country. We can learn something from them, too. Don't come in overnight and start advertising. Take your time. Plan your campaign carefully. Remember, there are millions of people in China who don't know what a Big Mac is. So don't rush over there and try to sell them one. Take your time. Think ahead five or ten years. It pays to be patient in China.

3   Now in Russia, you have to think about your product and whether or not there's a market for it. Take fast food, for example. In Russia, that's a very strange idea. In their restaurants, you sit down and the waiter brings you soup, salad, meat, potatoes— one thing at a time. The Russians think of food as something you take your time with, something you enjoy.

4   It's funny what happened with pizza in Russia. First they had to convince people to try it, and explain that it was similar to Russian *vatrushka*. Then Pizzaria restaurant opened up in Moscow. The Russians may have liked it all right, but Pizzaria didn't go over too well with foreign visitors. That's because the pizza didn't always have enough tomato sauce and cheese! Another problem was that if you wanted to take the pizza home with you, the chef wouldn't hear of it. He didn't want it to get cold. See? When you're dealing with international markets, you're dealing with other customs, other cultures.

5   But things are changing every day. New markets are opening up all the time. You have to look at the big picture before you start planning a campaign. Think about your product. Will people be able to buy it? Think about your marketing plan. Will people understand it? Remember that for years in China and Russia, people had a hard time buying things. The best advertisement of all was a long line in front of a store. That's how people knew which store was the place to go. So think about how things are changing. And thank you for being here today.

netscape 136.02
136.12

B. LINKING READINGS ONE AND TWO

1 *Imagine that you are an advertiser who read Julia Ross's speech in* Adworld. *What did you learn? How is this information related to the problems of global advertising that are described in Reading One? Consider such areas as laws, customs, and likes/dislikes.*

Complete the following letter with your own ideas.

01-12-99
Date

Dear Ms. Ross:

I recently read part of your speech in *Adworld.* I was especially interested to learn that _Your advertisment_ _was very insterting to all us_.

It was also interesting to hear that _you can_ _promoot this product_.

I have a few questions for you. _____

_____?

I have another question. _____

_____?

Thank you for taking the time to respond to my letter.

Sincerely,

Computer LAB.

Sticker

ATC

downstair

password

2 dream

2 *Work in pairs. Compare advertising in your home culture to advertising in another country. How do advertisers convince people to buy products? Are there any laws that advertisers must follow? What kinds of problems do you think advertisers have when they translate ads from other cultures into your home culture? Share your ideas with the class.*

REVIEWING LANGUAGE

A. EXPLORING LANGUAGE

Read each sentence. Look at the underlined words and the four choices below each sentence. Which of the choices is not related to the underlined word? Circle it. The first one has been done for you.

1. The <u>goal</u> of the advertising campaign was to sell more cars to women.

   a. purpose   c. hope
   b. plan   d. future

2. Women with young children are part of a growing <u>market</u>.

   a. group of people   c. group of buyers
   b. group of stores   d. group of customers

3. The ad's <u>message</u> was that the new cars were safe.

   a. idea   c. style
   b. information   d. story

4. The ads were <u>successful</u> because many women believed in the safety of the cars.

   a. effective   c. powerful
   b. certain   d. convincing

5. As a result, the ads <u>convinced</u> mothers to buy the cars.

   a. encouraged   c. taught
   b. pushed   d. told

6. However, the ads <u>failed</u> to sell cars to single women without children.

   a. didn't sell   c. were unable to sell
   b. couldn't sell   d. tried to sell

7. The advertising campaign will become <u>global</u> next year.

   a. multinational   c. organized
   b. worldwide   d. international

8. Ads for the <u>competition</u> will not become global.

   a. race   c. other sellers
   b. other companies   d. different firms

B. WORKING WITH WORDS

Idioms are phrases that have a special meaning. The meaning of the phrase is very different from the meanings of the words taken separately. Idioms are often used in conversation.

Listed below are sentences from Reading Two. Read the sentences and match the underlined idiom to the best definition.

a. said "no" strongly	**e.** very common
b. had difficulty	**f.** enter quickly
c. one after another	**g.** hurry
d. did not succeed	**h.** consider the general situation

_____ 1. In places like France and Spain, you'll watch at least a half hour of the program, then you'll get some commercials. <u>All in a row</u>.

_____ 2. Government advertising, yes—that was <u>all over the place.</u>

_____ 3. Don't <u>come in overnight</u> and start advertising. Take your time. Plan your campaign carefully.

_____ 4. Remember, there are millions of people in China who don't know what a Big Mac is. So don't <u>rush over</u> there and try to sell them one.

_____ 5. The Russians may have liked it all right, but Pizzaria <u>didn't go over too well</u> with foreign visitors.

_____ 6. Another problem was that if you wanted to take the pizza home with you, the chef <u>wouldn't hear of it</u>. He didn't want it to get cold.

_____ 7. New markets are opening up all the time. You have to <u>look at the big picture</u> before you start planning a campaign.

_____ 8. Remember that for years in China and Russia, people <u>had a hard time</u> buying things.

6 SKILLS FOR EXPRESSION

A. GRAMMAR: Contrast—Simple Present Tense and Present Progressive

1 *Read the description of a business meeting on page 15. Underline all the verbs. Then discuss these questions with the class.*

1. Which verbs describe actions that are taking place now?

2. What form do these verbs have?

3. Look at the nonaction verbs that express emotions or describe mental states. What form do these verbs have?

It's 7:00 P.M. The business people want to go home, but they cannot. They are having an important meeting. At this meeting, they are planning a television advertising campaign for a new fast-food restaurant, Veggie Delight. They hope to reach the young parents' market. Young parents are often busy and don't have time to cook. People in this market care about the health of their families. Right now, the business people are discussing ways to send the message that Veggie Delight offers healthy fast food. Several people are writing down ideas for the campaign.

Simple Present Tense and Present Progressive

FOCUS ON GRAMMAR

See Contrast: Simple Present Tense and Present Progressive in *Focus on Grammar, Intermediate.*

a. The **simple present tense** is used to describe what sometimes happens, what usually happens, or what always happens.

◆ Busy parents sometimes **buy** dinner at fast-food restaurants.

b. Nonaction verbs describe emotions, mental states, and situations.

◆ Some people **worry** that fast food is not good for their health. (emotion)

◆ Most people **believe** that home-cooked food is better for their health. (mental state)

◆ There **are** many television advertisements for fast-food restaurants. (situation)

c. The **present progressive tense** is used to describe actions that are happening at the present time.

◆ The business people **are having** an important meeting now.

◆ At the moment, some of them **are discussing** ideas for their campaign.

◆ At the same time, others **are listening** carefully and **writing down** ideas.

2 *Read the following sentences. Complete each one with the correct verb tense: simple present or present progressive. Use the choices below the blanks.*

1. Television ads for fast food always ___*makes*___ the food look

   (make/are making)

   delicious.

2. Some people today ___*are losing*___ the habit of cooking at home

   (lose/are losing)

   because they are busy.

3. Many of them ___*believe*___ that there is nothing wrong with

   (believe/are believing)

   eating fast food once in a while.

4. Nowadays, the number of fast-food restaurants around the world

   ___*is increasing*___

   (increases/is increasing)

5. These restaurants usually ___*serve*___ different foods in different

   (serve/are serving)

   parts of the world.

6. Many people ___*consider*___ McDonald's to be an excellent

   (consider/are considering)

   example of a successful global restaurant.

B. STYLE: Paragraph Development

1 *Read the following paragraph from "Advertising All Over the World." Then discuss the questions with the class.*

1. Where is the main idea?

2. Where are the examples?

3. How many examples are there?

   Global advertisers must also consider differences in laws and customs. For instance, certain countries will not allow TV commercials on Sunday, and others will not allow TV commercials for children's products on any day of the week. In some parts of the world, it is forbidden to show dogs on television or certain types of clothing, such as jeans. The global advertiser who does not understand such laws and customs will soon have problems.

Paragraph Structure

A paragraph usually presents one **main idea.** This idea appears at the beginning of a paragraph and is followed by one or more examples. The sentence that states the main idea is called a **topic sentence.** In many paragraphs, the topic sentence is the first sentence. Then the following sentences give examples to prove that the topic sentence is true or to discuss the topic in more detail. At the end of the paragraph, there is usually a **concluding sentence** that repeats key words from the topic sentence. Look at the following examples:

Topic Sentence: Global advertisers must consider differences in laws and customs.

- **Example 1:** Some countries do not allow TV advertisements on Sunday.

- **Example 2:** Other countries never allow TV advertisements for children's products.

- **Example 3:** In some parts of the world, dogs and jeans cannot be shown on television.

Concluding Sentence: The global advertiser who does not understand such laws and customs will soon have problems.

2 *Identify each sentence below as follows:*

TS = Topic Sentence ✓   **D1** = Detail 1 ✓
CS = Concluding Sentence ✓   **D2** = Detail 2 ✓
                                                D3 = Detail 3 ✓

Then write a paragraph by putting the sentences in order. Indent the first sentence.

___CS___ **1.** In addition, Veggie Delight serves potatoes that are baked, not fried in oil. ✓

___D1___ **2.** They can enjoy the tasty Veggie Burger, which contains no meat.

___D3___ **3.** They can also enjoy fresh juices instead of soft drinks.

___TS___ **4.** Busy families love to eat at Veggie Delight.

___D2___ **5.** Eating these foods is a healthy pleasure for busy families.

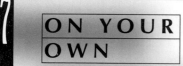

ON YOUR OWN

A. WRITING TOPICS

Choose one of the following topics and write a paragraph with a topic sentence, details, and a concluding sentence. Use some of the vocabulary, grammar, and style that you learned in this unit.

a. Think of an advertisement that you enjoy watching on TV. What is the message of this ad? How does it convince people to buy the product?

b. Do you agree with laws that forbid advertising campaigns for tobacco and alcohol? Explain your opinion.

c. Consider a time when you bought something because an advertisement convinced you to buy it. Were you disappointed with the product? Or were you happy with it?

B. FIELDWORK

1 *Look at billboard advertisements in your community. Choose one bill-board and complete the following worksheet.*

Type of product: _____

_____

Message (pictures, words, or both): _____

_____

Possible markets: _____

_____

Will the ad be successful?   Yes   No   Maybe

Explanation: _____

_____

_____

_____

2 *Next, work in a small group to combine all your information on the chart on the next page.*

3 *Finally, discuss whether or not these ads would be successful globally. To succeed in the global market, how would they have to be changed?*

	MESSAGE	MARKET	WILL THE AD SUCCEED?
Product 1			
Product 2			
Product 3			
Product 4			

TELECOMMUTING: GOING HOME TO WORK

1 APPROACHING THE TOPIC

A. PREDICTING

1 Look at the illustration. Read the title of the unit. Take five minutes to write your answers to the following questions. Where is the woman? What is she doing? Does she look happy? Why or why not?

2 Work in a small group. Discuss the following questions. Do you know anyone who works at home? What job does that person have? Would you like to have a job where you could work from home? Why or why not?

B. SHARING INFORMATION

Many working people have begun to telecommute. They now do some or most of their work at home. They use the telephone and computer to communicate and work with other people.

Work in a small group. Think about the type of work done by each of the following workers. Which workers must do their work out of the home, in an office, or in a public place? Which workers could do some of their work at home? Which workers could do most of their work at home? Check (✔) the category that best describes the situation.

JOB	ALWAYS WORKS OUTSIDE OF THE HOME	SOMETIMES WORKS AT HOME	MOSTLY WORKS AT HOME
1. Computer programmer			
2. Teacher			
3. Nurse			
4. Magazine editor			
5. Car mechanic			
6. Lawyer			
7. Waiter, waitress			
8. Clothing designer			

PREPARING TO READ

A. BACKGROUND

*Think about the advantages and disadvantages of telecommuting. How do you think **the employee, the employer,** and **society** might feel about telecommuting? Discuss your answers in groups. Take notes in the chart below.*

	THE EMPLOYEE (THE WORKER)	THE EMPLOYER (THE BOSS)	SOCIETY (PEOPLE IN GENERAL)
Advantages			
Disadvantages			

B. VOCABULARY FOR COMPREHENSION

Try to guess the meaning of these words from your knowledge of English, or use a dictionary. In each set of words, cross out the word or phrase that is not similar in meaning to the first word or phrase. Compare your answers with those of another student. Discuss the relationship between the words in each set.

Example

rural   countryside   rustic   ~~urban~~

Countryside and **rustic** both mean "outside of the city." They are similar in meaning to **rural**. Urban, however, means that something is in or near the city. You would cross out **urban** because it is not similar to **rural**.

1. *stressed*	tense	pressured	~~relaxed~~
2. *depressed*	stressed	sad	unhappy
3. *telecommuter*	person who works from home	person who seldom commutes to work	person who commutes to work
4. *flexible*	adjust	able to change	can't bend
5. *cure*	solution	answer	problem
6. *isolated*	joined	alone	separated
7. *cope with*	be afraid of	manage	deal with
8. *face-to-face*	over the phone	in person	in the same room
9. *relocate*	find something you lost	move to another place to live	change the city you live in because of work
10. *desocialize*	participate in society	not join in society	break away from society

READING ONE: Going Home to Work

A. INTRODUCING THE TOPIC

Read the first two paragraphs of the magazine article below. First write your answers to these questions. Then discuss your ideas with the class. What advantages might Helene McQuade have in staying home to work for her company? What disadvantages might she have?

_____

_____

_____

Now read the rest of the article.

Going Home to Work

1   "I felt I was spending my life on the road," said editor Helene McQuade. For five and a half years she spent three hours a day driving to and from her job at a magazine. When she married her husband, Jack, she moved into his home in the country. She did not want to quit her job, so she continued to work. But her office was in the city, 75 miles away. She left the house at 6:00 A.M. five days a week and got home each night at 7:30 P.M. By the time she got home each night, she felt tired, stressed, and depressed. And things only got worse when she and her husband had a baby.

2   McQuade finally decided to quit her job. But her boss asked her to continue working for the company. He said she could stay in the country and work at home. She only had to drive into the city once a week to pick up and deliver her work or attend meetings. McQuade agreed to try it.

3   Today fewer people in the United States drive to work. Like Helene McQuade, they have stopped commuting to work. They stay home. They have not lost their jobs or started their own companies—they are a new type of employee: the telecommuter. Over 5 million working people in the U.S. divide their work between home and the office. Some work mostly at home, some work mostly in the office, and some work at home half the time and in the office half the time. Today, with a modern system of communications, many people can work

anywhere. An individual only needs a supportive boss and a well-equipped office: a telephone and an answering machine, a computer and a printer, a copier, a fax machine, and a modem. Researchers predict that, in just a few years, 41 percent of workers in the United States will telecommute. Driving to work may soon become something from the past.

4 Employees like telecommuting because they can have a more flexible working schedule. They can start to work when they want. They can work in the evening and go out in the morning or the afternoon. They don't have to spend as much time sitting in highway traffic. They can take advantage of the fresh air. Moreover, telecommuting gives working mothers and fathers more time with their families.

5 But telecommuting is not the cure for all working people who feel stressed in their jobs. People who work at home alone often feel isolated. They seldom see people face-to-face. With less time in the office, they may spend most of their working hours alone. They usually spend more time in contact with machines than with human beings, so they sometimes feel lonely.

6 In fact, not everyone makes a good telecommuter. People who telecommute need to make their own work schedule. Some telecommuters report that they work more hours when they are in the comfort of their own homes. In fact, they sometimes think their home is work, and this makes them feel confused. When home and work get confused, people feel as if they never leave work. Some families have problems coping with work at home. For example, the children may not understand that they cannot talk to mom (or dad) when she (or he) is working. In addition, not all jobs or professions can allow telecommuting. An editor of a magazine may be able to spend most of the time working at home. A hospital nurse or school teacher, however, may not.

7 Employers may not accept the idea of telecommuting, either. They may feel a loss of control over employees who work at home. Also, employers often believe that the best work gets done when people work with people. Face-to-face meetings are not possible with telecommuters. Meetings on the phone are not the same. The subtle messages of body language get lost in phone discussions. In addition, when employees work at home, it is not possible to solve problems that need immediate attention. The biggest problem, in fact, may be trust. Can an employer trust the employee to do his or her work without a manager watching? The employer must choose the right person to telecommute.

8 Yet if employers can manage feeling a loss of control over employees, they may find many advantages. Telecommuting can save money for a business. Running an office will be less expensive if people work at home. Employees will be happier and, as a result, more productive. A California study showed that telecommuters were 20 percent more productive than office workers. Actually, many telecommuters report working ten-hour days, rather than eight-hour days, when they work at home. Another advantage for employers is that they can hire more employees who cannot relocate. If an employee cannot move to where the company is, he or she can telecommute. They can also keep employees who might want to leave the company because of long commutes. If a company can keep its employees, it can save on the money that would be needed to train new employees.

9 The benefits of telecommuting may be even greater for society. If more people work at home, there will be fewer cars on the highways. If there are fewer cars on the highways, there will be less gasoline used and less pollution. In addition, if people are able to work at home, more women and workers with disabilities can be hired. As families balance the demands of work and family life, they will be happier and more productive.

10 But again, is telecommuting the perfect solution for society? As people have more

opportunities to work at home, many may move to the suburbs or to rural areas. As they move out of the cities, the cities will be left without their employed population. The unemployed people who stay in the cities will not pay taxes to the cities. Therefore there will be less money to maintain the cities' roads, water supply, electric supply, and so on.

11   There is a more serious problem than maintaining the cities. As people become more comfortable working alone, they may become less social. It's easier to stay home in comfortable exercise clothes or a bathrobe than to get dressed for yet another business meeting!

12   "I am happy to keep my job and work at home," says Helene McQuade, "but I feel isolated from my colleagues in the office." Spending more time with machines than people may also add to this social problem. It has been shown that people have become less polite in their electronic mail (e-mail) communications.

13   Both the crumbling, or breaking down, of our cities and the desocializing of society are not small problems as we consider the possibility of telecommuting.

B. READING FOR MAIN IDEAS

*Read each statement and decide if it is true or false. Write **T** or **F**.*

_____ **1.** Helene McQuade has become a telecommuter.

_____ **2.** More and more people in the United States are telecommuting.

_____ **3.** Telecommuting is the perfect solution for all employees.

_____ **4.** Some employers think there are problems with telecommuting.

_____ **5.** Telecommuting is helpful to the environment.

_____ **6.** Socializing will increase with telecommuting.

C. READING FOR DETAILS

Read the questions. Circle the best answer. Write the number of the paragraph where you found the answer.

Paragraph

1. How did Helene McQuade feel about her job in the city? _____
   a. She didn't like her boss.
   b. She didn't like her job.
   c. She didn't like driving to work.

2. What new group is staying home these days? _____
   a. People who are unemployed.
   b. People who have started their own businesses.
   c. Telecommuters.

3. What arrangements do telecommuters make with their employers? _____
   a. They do all their work at home.
   b. They do some work at home, some in the office.
   c. They do all their work in the office.

4. Which is not needed for a telecommuter's home office? _____
   a. Paper shredder
   b. Fax machine
   c. Telephone

5. Why might employees want to telecommute? _____
   a. They don't have to see their boss so often.
   b. They can find better child-care services.
   c. They can have a better work schedule.

6. Why might employees *not* want to telecommute? _____
   a. They make less money.
   b. They don't spend as much time with their families.
   c. They may work more.

7. Why might employers dislike telecommuting? _____
   a. They have less control over their employees.
   b. They can't easily call their employees on the telephone.
   c. They have face-to-face meetings.

Paragraph

8. Why might employers benefit from telecommuting?   _____
   a. They will need fewer employees.
   b. They will keep their employees.
   c. They can retrain employees more easily.

9. With telecommuting, what will happen to cars?   _____
   a. They will be more common on the highways.
   b. They will use more gasoline.
   c. They will produce less air pollution.

10. What is a disadvantage of telecommuting?   _____
    a. Risk of crumbling cities
    b. More business meetings to attend
    c. Communication with e-mail

D. READING BETWEEN THE LINES

1 *Work in groups. Read the questions. Discuss your answers.*

Look back at your list of the advantages and disadvantages of telecommuting in section 3A. What information did the reading have that matched your ideas? What other information did the reading have?

2 *Read the questions and possible answers. Look at Reading One again to find information to help you answer the questions. What are the most likely answers in your opinion? Discuss your answers.*

1. What did Helene McQuade mean by "I felt like I was spending my life on the road"?

   a. She spent too much time in her car.

   b. She didn't like to drive.

   c. She was getting old too fast.

2. Why did McQuade finally want to quit her job?

   a. Her husband could support the family.

   b. She couldn't find anyone to care for her child.

   c. She was tired from trying both to commute and to care for her baby.

3. Why didn't people telecommute years ago?

   a. Their bosses didn't allow it.

   b. They liked living close to their work.

   c. They didn't have the necessary office equipment.

4. Why do some families have problems coping with telecommuting?

   a. They get bored spending so much time together at home.

   b. They don't spend as much time in family activities as they would like.

   c. They don't get enough done.

5. What kind of subtle message may not get across in a telephone discussion?

   a. Looking at one's watch because of boredom.

   b. Raising one's voice because of anger.

   c. Asking thoughtful questions because of interest.

6. What is the biggest advantage of telecommuting to employers?

   a. Their employees spend more time with their families.

   b. It saves money for the company.

   c. They don't have to manage their employees as much.

7. Why does Helene McQuade feel isolated from her colleagues?

   a. She has a new baby, and they don't.

   b. She works harder than they do.

   c. She doesn't work as closely with them on projects.

8. Who is most accepting of telecommuting today?

   a. The telecommuter

   b. The employer of the telecommuter

   c. Society

4 READING TWO: Help Wanted

A. EXPANDING THE TOPIC

1 *The following abbreviations appear in the ads in the next reading. They are typically used in "help wanted" ads. Work with another student. Try to guess their meanings. Then look at the list of vocabulary below. Choose the correct word for each abbreviation and write it in the blank.*

1. Admin _____

2. Asst _____

3. co. _____

4. exp. _____

5. indiv. _____

6. ins. _____

7. MGR _____

8. Min. _____

9. nec _____

10. w/ _____

11. WP _____

12. yrs. _____

minimum	years	assistant
company	necessary	word processing
with	administrative	experience
insurance	individual	manager

2 *Work in groups. Read the following ads from the "help wanted" section of the newspaper. Answer the questions under each ad. Then decide if the job could offer the employee the opportunity to telecommute. Circle **Y** (yes) or **N** (no). Discuss your opinions.*

Vocabulary

in-house: located or done inside a business or company

sales rep: sales representative—a person whose job is to sell things for a company, either in a store or directly to the customer

1.

Admin Asst   Mid 30s
COOKS TODAY
Assistant to publisher of Gourmet Food magazine. Looking for indiv. w/strong communication skills. Challenging & creative projects! Type & WP. Call Sunday & Weekdays. Call 390-523-8990 or fax resume to 390-523-4367.

a. How much money will this job pay?

_____

b. Which office skills must the person have?

_____

c. Telecommuting possibilities?
   Y N

2.

Computer
TECHNICIAN
(IN-HOUSE)
In-house technician needed for growing media co. Repair and install computers and printers in a unique environment. Min. 2 yrs. exp. Contact Steve Gutman. Phone 552-9088. Fax 552-9612.

a. How many years of experience must the person have?

_____

b. What kind of company is this?

_____

c. Telecommuting possibilities?
   Y N

3.

Banking
ASST BRANCH MGR

Savings bank has a great opportunity for motivated indiv w/minimum 2 yrs. exp. Qualified candidates must be knowledgeable in banking policies and procedures. Excellent benefits package available. Send resume to: Midway Savings Bank, PO Box 577, Waterbury, MN 56778

a. What kind of person does the bank want?

_____

b. How many years experience must the person have?

_____

c. Telecommuting possibilities?
Y   N

4.

PRODUCTION EDITOR

Take responsibility for a monthly growing high-tech publication. Work closely with writers, designers, sales team, advertising agencies, and printer. Possibilities for some production work at home. Must be experienced in proofreading, copy editing and magazine layout. Send resume and letter to New Wave Magazine, 8 North Drive, Suite 280, Cedar Hills, NY 12401

a. How often is the magazine published?

_____

b. How many departments will this editor work with?

_____

c. Telecommuting possibilities?
Y   N

5.

BILINGUAL

Long-distance phone carrier seeks bilingual sales reps for the tri-state area. No experience nec - we will train. MUST be fluent in one or more of the following languages:
• Japanese   • Chinese
• Korean   • Haitian
• Spanish
Salary range $5-10/hr + commission.
308-399-8900
(fax) 308-399-7761

a. What will the bilingual sales representative sell?

_____

b. How much experience is necessary for the job?

_____

c. Telecommuting possibilities?
Y   N

6.

WORD PROCESSING EXPERTS

Leading financial firm needs expert word processors for 6-month project working days, nights, or weekends. Work WP Center. Exp. w/tables and charts nec. $18-23 per hr. Medical ins. available. Call Stuart, Mon.-Fri. at 908-7778 or fax 908-

a. What skills are necessary for this job?

_____

b. When will the person work?

_____

c. Telecommuting possibilities?
Y   N

B. LINKING READINGS ONE AND TWO

1 *Look at Reading One again. Read the paragraphs that explain some of the challenges telecommuters can face. With your class, make a list of those challenges. Then brainstorm about what type of person would like telecommuting and what type would not. What are the characteristics of each?*

Challenges Telecommuters Face

_____

_____

_____

_____

_____

CHARACTERISTICS OF A PERSON WHO WOULD LIKE TELECOMMUTING	CHARACTERISTICS OF A PERSON WHO WOULD NOT LIKE TELECOMMUTING

2 *Look at the "help wanted" ads again. You chose the jobs you believed could be done by a telecommuter. What are the characteristics of a job that would be more appropriate for telecommuting? Would you like telecommuting? Why or why not? Discuss your ideas with the class.*

5 REVIEWING LANGUAGE

A. EXPLORING LANGUAGE

Read the statements about telecommuting. Match each statement with the person you think would be most likely to make it.

_____ 1. "I love having him home more, but every time we sit down to dinner the phone rings."

_____ 2. "It will save on our training costs, but I'm not sure I want to start this year."

_____ 3. "I spend about 45 minutes driving to work each day, but it's worth it to live in the suburbs."

_____ 4. "We need to find ways to reduce the number of cars on the highways."

_____ 5. "I'm working more than ever before, but at least I get to see my kids grow up."

_____ 6. "I'm really happy that she doesn't have to spend so much time in her car."

a. A commuter

b. A telecommuter

c. An employer who is considering telecommuting

d. The wife of a telecommuter

e. Jack McQuade, Helene's husband

f. A government official

B. WORKING WITH WORDS

Analyze the relationships among the vocabulary from this unit. Choose the word below that best completes each analogy. Be sure that the second pair of words has a similar relationship to the first pair of words. Circle the correct answer. Then fill in the blanks to show the relationship. The first one has been done for you.

1. telecommuter : magazine editor :: commuter: <u>hospital nurse</u>

   employer   society   (hospital nurse)

   An example of a telecommuter is a magazine editor. An example of a commuter is a <u>hospital nurse</u>.

2. rural life : city life :: fresh air: _____

   indoor lighting   indoor air   sunny room

   Rural life is the opposite of city life. Fresh air is the opposite of _____ .

3. stressed : depressed :: isolated: _____

   flexible   cure   lonely

   Being stressed makes a person feel depressed. Being isolated makes a person feel _____ .

4. fax machine : telephone :: e-mail: _____

   modem   answering machine   copier

   To use a fax machine you need a telephone. To use e-mail you need a _____ .

5. telecommuting : future :: commuting: _____

   on the road   flexible working schedule   past

   Telecommuting is becoming a part of the future. Commuting is becoming a part of the _____ .

6. cope with : manage :: move: _____

relocate   trust   confuse

Cope with means the same as manage. Move means the same as
_____ .

7. body language : subtle message :: e-mail: _____

telephone message   copiers   computer message

Body language communicates a subtle message. E-mail communicates a _____ .

8. breaking down : crumbling :: disconnected: _____

on the road   alone   loss of control

Breaking down means the same as crumbling. Disconnected means the same as _____ .

9. cars on the highways : pollution :: people working at home:
_____

desocializing of society   telecommuters   supportive employers

Cars on the highways cause pollution. People working at home cause the _____ .

10. Ten-hour work days : telecommuting :: less polite communications:
_____

face-to-face meetings   e-mail   crumbling cities

Ten-hour work days are characteristic of telecommuting. Less polite communications are characteristic of _____ .

6 SKILLS FOR EXPRESSION

A. GRAMMAR: Modals and Related Verbs That Show Ability

1 *Look at the following examples. Work with a partner. Can you paraphrase these sentences?*

◆ Employees like telecommuting because they *can* have a more flexible working schedule.

◆ She *could* stay home in the country and work in her home office.

◆ If people *are able to* work at home, more women and disabled workers *can* be hired.

◆ Employers will *be able to* save more money.

FOCUS ON GRAMMAR

See Modals and Related Verb Forms That Show Ability in *Focus on Grammar, Intermediate.*

Modals and Related Verbs That Show Ability

a. Use *can* to talk about ability in the present.
  ◆ I **can** drive a car.

b. Use *be able to* to talk about ability in the present or the future.
  ◆ I **am able to** work at home. (Present)
  ◆ I'm **not able to** work at home. (Negative present)
  ◆ I **will be able to** work at home with my new job. (Future)

c. Use *could* or *was/were able to* to talk about general ability in the past.
  ◆ I **could** spend two hours commuting. Now I work at home; I spend little time in my car. (Past)
  ◆ I **was able to** buy a cheap computer for my home office. (Past)
  ◆ I **wasn't able to** buy a cheap computer for my home office. (Past negative)

d. The modals *can* and *could* have only one form. To talk about ability in tenses other than present (*can*) or past (*could*) it is necessary to use *be able to*.
  ◆ He wants to **be able to** work at home.
  ◆ She has **been able to** work at home.

2 *When Helene McQuade started to telecommute, she wrote a letter to her friend Barbara. Fill in the blanks with the verb of ability that best fits the sentence. Use* **can, can't, could, couldn't,** *and* **be able to.**

March 13

Dear Barbara,

Thank you for your letter. I was hoping to hear from you. I'm glad to hear you and Aaron are doing well and that you (**1**) _____ visit us this summer.

You want to know when I will (**2**) _____ leave my job. You're right . . . the commute is really too much. But, when I told my boss I had decided to quit, he asked me to stay. He said he would make it easier for me to do my job, so now I (**3**) _____ do most of my work from home! I'm much happier at home with Jack and the baby.

You probably think I (**4**) _____ get much work done at home since I'm writing you this letter. All my friends think that. But you'd be surprised. Actually, I (**5**) _____ get much more done than when I was in the office. I (**6**) _____ concentrate on my work more easily because there aren't as many interruptions. I just (**7**) _____ get anything done in the office. I never realized how much time I wasted in office gossip!

The worst part of working at home is that I miss my friends in the office. It can be lonelier working at home. But I still drive into the office once a week. I (**8**) _____ always have lunch with Terry or June while I'm there.

I'm sorry that Jack and I will not (**9**) _____ see you next week at my mom's place for Easter. However, I'm sure we'll (**10**) _____ catch up on everything when you come in the summer. With my new job arrangements, I should be able to take a few days off. Give me a call when you know your plans.

Write soon!

Love,

Helene

B. STYLE: Letter Writing

❶ *Look at the letter in Section 6A. A letter usually has six basic parts. Which parts do you recognize?*

❷ *Read the following information about each part of a letter.*

The **date:** In the United States, the date is written in this order: month, day, year.

The **recipient's address:** This is used in business letters. Personal letters, like the one in Section 6A, do not generally include this.

The **salutation:** This part opens the letter. It usually begins with "Dear . . ."

The **body:** This is the main part of the letter. It includes one or more paragraphs.

The **close:** This is the expression we use to finish the letter, before signing our name.

The **signature:** If the letter is typed, this is always written by hand, in ink. In formal letters, the person's name, title, and company are typed below the signature.

---

❸ *Label each part of Helene McQuade's letter on page 39.*

❹ *Read the help wanted ad for **Production Editor** on page 33 again. Then read the following letter of application. How is a business letter, which is more formal, different from a personal letter? Work in groups. Discuss your answers to these questions.*

1. Where does the date appear in a business letter? Where are the margins?

2. Which address appears in a business letter but is not necessary in a personal letter?

3. How is the salutation different from a personal letter?

4. How is the closing more formal than in a personal letter?

5. What appears under McQuade's name in a business letter?

January 31, 1999

New Wave Magazine
8 North Drive, Suite 280
Cedar Hills, NY 12401

To whom it may concern:

I am responding to your ad for a Production Editor in last week's *Advocate*.

As you will see from my resume, I have several years of experience as a production editor. I have experience in proofreading and copy editing for a variety of publications, from medical journals to technology newsletters. I also did full-time layout work when I worked for a monthly sports magazine. My experience is varied. I feel I have the skills for your position.

I am currently the managing editor of McDermott Publishers. I manage thirteen employees as well as edit educational brochures. Since I had a baby six months ago, I have found it difficult to continue in a management position. I would like to return to production editing. I am particularly interested in the possibility of doing some work at home, as mentioned in your ad.

Could I request an interview at your convenience? I would be interested in talking more with you about the position.

I look forward to hearing from you.

Sincerely,

Helene McQuade

Helene McQuade
Managing Editor
McDermott Publishers

5 *The following letter of application is incomplete. Imagine that you are applying for the **Assistant Branch Manager**'s job you read about in the ad on page 33. Fill in the missing parts of the letter to make it complete.*

[Date]   _____

[Recipient's address]   Midway Savings Bank

                                    _____

                                    Waterbury, MN 56778

[Salutation]   To whom _____:

[Body]   I am responding to your ad _____ in yesterday's *New York Times*.

                                    As you can see from my resume, _____ _____ .
I have experience in _____ . I also
_____ . Since I have exactly the type of experience your ad mentioned, I feel I have the skills for your position.

                                    I am currently the head teller at Riverland Savings Bank. I manage
_____ . In addition, _____ . I am looking for the opportunity to improve _____
_____ . Your bank would be the ideal situation for me.

[Close]   I would like to request _____ . I would be interested in _____ .

                                    I look forward _____ .

                                    _____ ,

[Signature]   _____
                                    Riverland Savings Bank

ON YOUR OWN

A. WRITING TOPICS

Choose one of the following topics. Write two or three paragraphs using some of the vocabulary, grammar, and style that you learned in this unit.

a. Imagine that you are a manager with five employees who telecommute. Write a letter to your local newspaper explaining why you don't like managing telecommuters. What are the problems for you and the company?

b. How will technology change the way you work ten or fifteen years from now? Write a paragraph in which you imagine the working world of the future. Will people still drive to work? How will communication change between co-workers and managers?

c. Write a letter to your boss explaining why you would like to telecommute. Tell him or her why you think you would be a better employee and why this would be better for the company.

B. FIELDWORK

Prepare to interview a person who telecommutes. Follow the steps below.

Step 1: With a partner, brainstorm questions you would like to ask in the interview. Look back at "Going Home to Work" to get ideas for your questions. Here are some examples:

- ◆ How long have you been telecommuting?
- ◆ Why did you decide to telecommute?
- ◆ What do you like about being a telecommuter?
- ◆ What do you dislike about being a telecommuter?
- ◆ Would you like to continue being a telecommuter? Why or why not?
- ◆ Has telecommuting changed the way you communicate? If yes, how?

Step 2: With the whole class, make an interview form to use for the interview.

Step 3: Do the interview.

Step 4: Compare your answers with those of the other students.

miracol

A MIRACLE CURE?

Lose the Fat around Your Waist and in Your Belly Now
Lose up to 5 inches in only 50 days!

Get that sculptured, hard look that women love. Men who use Sculptured Body can lose up to 5 inches from their belly in 50 days or less—without even exercising! Sculptured Body contains only organic ingredients that help you lose the fat. Available to you by calling 1-800-555-5555. Sculptured Body guarantees you will have the body women love, or your money back.

APPROACHING THE TOPIC

A. PREDICTING Look at the advertisement. Discuss these questions with the class.

1. What does the product in the ad promise to do?

2. Do you think it works? Why or why not?

3. Do you know anyone who has ever used a product like this? What happened?

B. SHARING INFORMATION

A **treatment** is a way to cure a sickness or to improve a person's health. Below is a chart with several different treatments and space at the bottom for you to write a treatment you've tried. Interview a partner about the treatments and fill in the chart with information about your partner. Check (✔) the appropriate columns. Discuss your answers with the class.

TREATMENT	HE/SHE HAS SEEN ADS ON TV OR IN MAGAZINES.	HE/SHE HAS USED IT OR KNOWS SOMEONE WHO HAS USED IT.	IT WORKED.	IT DIDN'T WORK.
1. An herb tea to cure a cold	*Doctor gave her for medice* ✔			
2. A drink for quick weight loss	✔			
3. A cream to grow hair			✔	✔
4. A cream to remove wrinkles			✔	
5. A vitamin to cure cancer				✔
6. Herbs to cure arthritis				
7. Tiger bone to increase strength				
8. _Soup_				

2 PREPARING TO READ

A. BACKGROUND

1 *Think about what you discussed in Section 1B and read the statements below.*

Facts about Quackery*

- ◆ Americans spend 27 billion dollars a year getting their medical treatment from quacks (people who sell health products or treatments that don't work).

- ◆ Thirty-eight million Americans have used a quack's products or treatments in the past year.

- ◆ One out of ten people who uses a quack's products is hurt in some way.

- ◆ Sixty percent of the people hurt by quacks are elderly.

- ◆ Quack clinics are often located outside of the United States.

- ◆ Americans spend 2 billion dollars a year on quack arthritis cures.

- ◆ Arthritis affects 40 million Americans. Ninety-five percent try treatments that are not proven to be true.

2 *Discuss these questions with another student.*

1. Some people don't go to a doctor when they are sick. They go to a person who gives them a treatment they believe will help them. Why do many people want to avoid going to a doctor?

2. Why do you think quack clinics are located outside the United States?

3. From the facts above, we learn that quacks sell more than half of their products to the elderly. Why do you think the elderly buy these products?

---

*Quackery: the practice of pretending to have medical knowledge or pretending to be able to cure diseases.

B. VOCABULARY FOR COMPREHENSION

Read each item below. Then choose the best definition for the underlined word in the sentence.

1. Hi, my name is Anne. I'm depressed because I recently lost a lot of money. I was the <u>victim</u> of a quack.

   A victim is . . .

   a. a person who is hurt or destroyed by someone or something else.

   b. a person who is helped by someone or something else.

   c. a person who wants to help someone or something else.

2. Here's what happened. I wanted to get a job as a flight attendant on an airplane. The problem is that I had to lose ten pounds within one week to be able to get the job. It seemed impossible. Then I saw an ad in the newspaper for a quick weight-loss product. The ad said I could lose fourteen pounds in one week! It seemed like a <u>miracle</u> because I could lose the ten pounds and get the job.

   A miracle is . . .

   a. a normal event.

   b. a surprising and wonderful event.

   c. an impossible event.

3. The quick weight-loss product was a drink. The drink was the <u>discovery</u> of a man who went to the Amazon jungle. Some Indians living in the jungle taught him how to make the drink. They had been making this drink for hundreds of years.

   A discovery is . . .

   a. finding something that was lost.

   b. finding something that nobody knew about before.

   c. finding something in another country.

medical

ar-thri-tis

miracle

can cer (sir)

cancel

unfortunaly

quackery

4. The man who discovered the drink was John Zimmerman. He had a <u>clinic</u> that people could stay at for one week to lose weight.

A clinic is . .

a. a place where people go to learn something.

b. a place where people go to relax.

c. a place where people go to receive medical advice or treatment.

5. If a person went to Mr. Zimmerman's clinic, Mr. Zimmerman <u>guaranteed</u> that the person would lose fourteen pounds. If the person didn't lose fourteen pounds, Mr. Zimmerman would give back the money he or she paid to come to the clinic.

To guarantee something means to . . .

a. make something better.

b. advertise something.

c. promise that something will work.

6. Mr. Zimmerman was also <u>offering</u> a special price for one month only. The treatment would only cost $2,000 instead of $3,000.

To offer something means to . . .

a. provide it.

b. loan it.

c. keep it.

7. My parents didn't want me to buy this treatment because it was <u>unproven</u>.

When something is unproven it . . .

a. can't be sold.

b. is inexpensive.

c. has not been shown to be true.

8. But I wanted my father to buy this product because it also helps <u>arthritis</u>. My father has a lot of pain in his hands and shoulders. If you take the drink for two weeks, you will not have arthritis pain for one year.

Arthritis is . . .

a. a condition in which a person's joints are swollen and painful.

b. a condition in which a person can't see well.

c. a condition in which a person can't eat very much.

9. I paid the $2,000 and received the drinks. Unfortunately, I didn't lose any weight at all. When I tried to call the clinic, I found out the phone had been disconnected. The clinic was not real and the drink didn't work. I had been the victim of health <u>fraud</u>.

An example of fraud is . . .

a. helping people who are sick.

b. getting money by lying to someone.

c. learning how to cure people.

10. The drink was <u>harmless</u>, but I lost $2,000!

If something is harmless . . .

a. it won't hurt you.

b. it isn't real.

c. it won't make you gain weight.

READING ONE: A Miracle Cure?

A. INTRODUCING THE TOPIC

The following article is taken from a popular magazine. Discuss these questions with your class.

1. Read the title. Why is the title a question? What is "a miracle cure"? Can you think of examples of miracle cures from your own life?

2. Read the first paragraph of "A Miracle Cure?" If you were Matt, would you do what he did? Why or why not?

A Miracle Cure?

1   One year ago, Matt Bloomfield was told he had cancer. His doctors decided to treat his cancer immediately. A few months after the treatments, however, Matt found out that the cancer was still growing. He became sick and depressed. Because he always had pain, the doctors gave him more medicine, but it didn't help. Finally, the doctors told him that they couldn't do anything more; he had only six months to live. Matt would do anything to save his life. He went to see a doctor who turned out to be a real quack.

2   More and more people are turning away from their doctors and, instead, going to individuals who have no medical training and who sell unproven treatments. They go to quacks to get everything from treatments for colds to cures for cancer. And they are putting themselves in dangerous situations.

3   Many people don't realize how unsafe it is to use unproven treatments. First of all, the treatments usually don't work. They may be harmless, but, if someone uses these products instead of proven treatments, he or she may be harmed. Why? Because during the time the person is using the product, his or her illness may be getting worse. This can even cause the person to die.

4   So why do people trust quacks? People want the "miracle cure." They want the product that will solve their problem . . . quickly, easily, and completely. A patient may be so afraid of pain, or even of dying, that he or she will try anything. The quack knows this and offers an easy solution at a very high price.

5   Quacks usually sell products and treatments for illnesses that generally have no proven cure. This is why we often hear about clinics that treat cancer or AIDS. Treatments for arthritis are also popular with quacks. Other common quackeries are treatments to lose weight quickly, to make hair grow again, and to keep a person young.

6   How can you recognize a quack? Sometimes it's easy because he or she offers something we know is impossible. A drink to keep you young is an example of this. But many times, these people lie, saying that their product was made because of a recent scientific discovery. This makes it more difficult to know if the person is real or a fraud. Another way to recognize quackery is that many quacks will say their product is good for many different illnesses, not just for one thing. They usually like to offer money-back guarantees if their treatment doesn't work. Unfortunately, the guarantee is often also a lie. Finally, the fraudulent clinic will often be in another country. Laws in the United States will not allow a quack to have a clinic in the United States because the quack doesn't have the proper medical training.

7   Quacks try to sell their products in similar ways. They will invite you to read testimonials, letters written by satisfied customers. These frauds will also promise quick, exciting cures. Often they say the product is made in a secret way or with something secret in it which can only be bought from a particular company. Quacks will also say that doctors and the rest of the medical community are against them.

8   There are some things you can do to protect yourself from health fraud. Before you buy a product or treatment, check to

see if it's the real thing. Talk to a doctor, pharmacist, or another health professional. If you've been the victim of health fraud, you can complain to certain organizations. In the United States, the Better Business Bureau, the Food and Drug Administration (FDA), the Federal Trade Commission, or the National Council against Health Fraud will help you.

9   Don't let yourself or anyone you know become a victim of health fraud. It could cost you a lot of money or, worse yet, your life.

B. READING FOR MAIN IDEAS

Read the main ideas from Reading One. A word is missing from each sentence. Fill in the blank with the word that correctly completes the main idea. Label each main idea with the number of the paragraph it describes. The first one has been done for you.

Paragraph

1. The way that different quacks try to sell their products is often _____similar_____ .   _____7_____

   a. similar

   b. different

   c. varied

2. It's _____ to use a quack's products.   _____

   a. fun

   b. illegal

   c. dangerous

3. Quacks want to sell products for illnesses that have no _____ because their products don't really work.   _____

   a. medications

   b. cure

   c. side effects

4. If you are _____ about buying something from a quack, there are people and organizations that can help you.   _____

   a. excited

   b. worried

   c. satisfied

Paragraph

5. There are many things a person can look for to
   determine if a _____ is real or comes
   from a quack.   _____

   a. product

   b. secret

   c. salesman

6. People will often go to a quack because they want
   an easy answer for their _____ .   _____

   a. child

   b. customer

   c. problem

C. READING FOR DETAILS

*Read the paraphrased details from Reading One. Match the beginning of
the sentence on the left with the end of the sentence on the right. Then
match the details with the correct main idea in Section 3B. The first one
has been done for you.*

___g, 3___ **1.** Since AIDS has no cure,
. . .

a. is by offering a quick solution to
a problem.

_____ **2.** Quacks often lie about
their . . .

b. and will buy anything that
might be a cure.

_____ **3.** People go to quacks to
get . . .

c. to be sure it's not a quackery.

_____ **4.** You can ask a doctor
about a product . . .

d. a variety of treatments.

e. while using a quack's product.

_____ **5.** Quacks understand
that sick people are
often afraid of death
. . .

f. product or treatment.

_____ **6.** A person's illness could
get worse . . .

g. the treatment for it is a popular
quackery.

_____ **7.** One way that a quack
gets customers . . .

D. READING BETWEEN THE LINES

Imagine that your best friend, Joseph, is twenty-five years old—and going bald. He really wants to have more hair. He recently saw someone selling a shampoo that makes hair grow back in six months. It is made from a very unusual plant in the rain forest. He wants to buy this product, but he doesn't have enough money. He has asked you to loan him the money. He needs $1,000 for a six-month supply. You suspect this product is fraudulent. Look at "A Miracle Cure?" again. What are some of the ways you can tell if a person or product is a quack? Prepare a list of questions to ask Joseph about the product to determine if it's a quackery or not. The first one has been done for you.

1. <u>Did the person selling the product say that the product is based on a recent scientific discovery?</u> _____

2. _____

3. _____

4. _____

5. _____

6. _____

7. _____

4 READING TWO: The Organic Health Center

A. EXPANDING THE TOPIC

1 *Read the following advertisement about the Organic Health Center.*

The Organic Health Center

1   Do you have cancer? Have the doctors given you no hope? I can help you. My name is Benjamin Harrison. I am the founder[1] of the Organic Health Center. My health center specializes[2] in curing cancer and other diseases.

2   After traveling around the world for nine years looking for a cure for myself, I was able to learn the causes of cancer. Now, I can help others by offering them a cure. This cure is available only at the Organic Health Center.

3   As a result of my experiences, I realized that Western doctors are unqualified to help their patients. I, on the other hand, have learned how to use herbs[3] and organic[4] foods to heal, and I *am* qualified[5] to help you. That's why doctors will tell you not to trust me. They know that I can do something they can't do.

4   My program focuses on the whole body. It works on the cause of the cancer. I will put you on a healthy diet. The diet uses herb and plant products I have gathered from my travels around the world. All of the products I use are natural, so they won't make you feel sick. After one to six months, you will be cured of cancer.

5   Here are some of the programs my center offers:

PROGRAM A: **For all types of cancers**

You will stay at my clinic for one month of treatment. Then, you will continue the treatment in your home for two more months.

PROGRAM B: **For cancer detected early**

A sixty-day program done in your home. You will eat a special diet with herbs and other healthy foods. You will also follow an exercise schedule.

PROGRAM C: **For all other diseases**

A ninety-day program done in your home. You will eat a special diet with herbs and other healthy foods.

6   I am willing to travel to your home to teach you how to follow the program. And, if you would like, I have testimonial letters for you to read.

7   I provide a money-back guarantee if the program fails. Why? The money-back guarantee is my guarantee to you that my treatment works. A doctor will tell you that cancer can't be cured. It's the doctors who are the frauds.

---

[1] *founder:* the person who started something
[2] *specialize:* to have special knowledge and skill in something
[3] *herbs:* plants that can be used for cooking or medicine
[4] *organic:* plants and animals grown naturally without chemicals
[5] *qualified:* to be properly trained in something

2 *Answer the following questions. Then discuss your answers with a classmate.*

1. In one sentence, write what Reading Two is about.

2. How is Benjamin Harrison qualified to cure people who have cancer?

3. Explain his treatment for cancer.

B. LINKING READINGS ONE AND TWO

1 *Look at "A Miracle Cure?" again. Find the different ways to identify a quack. List them on the left side of the chart. Then read "The Organic Health Center" again. Look for examples that show that Benjamin Harrison might be a quack. Make a list of those examples below. Give the paragraph number where you found the example. The first one has been done for you.*

ITEM FROM "A MIRACLE CURE?" THAT IDENTIFIES A QUACK	EXAMPLE OF THAT ITEM FOUND IN "THE ORGANIC HEALTH CENTER"
1. They treat illnesses that generally have no cure.	__1__ 1. "My health center specializes in curing cancer and other diseases."
2.	_____ 2.
3.	_____ 3.
4.	_____ 4.
5.	_____ 5.
6.	_____ 6.
7.	_____ 7.

2 *Below are several treatments for cancer. Which ones do you think are real treatments (RT) and which ones are fraudulent (FT)? Discuss your answers with another student.*

_____ 1. A diet based on a new scientific discovery. It must be followed strictly for three months. The diet includes fruits, vegetables, nuts, and grains. Animal products such as meat, eggs, milk, and cheese cannot be eaten at all.

_____ 2. A series of acupuncture treatments. These are taken until the cancer disappears completely.

_____ 3. Radiation treatment on the part of the body where the cancer is growing. These treatments must be taken every day for four weeks.

_____ 4. Herbal treatment requires seven secret herbs to be cooked into the food at each meal. Meals must be taken six times a day until the cancer disappears.

_____ 5. Intensive exercise program with special tea. This treatment must be followed exactly for six months. A special herbal tea made from the bark of Brazilian trees is taken before and after each exercise session. The exercises clean out the body so that the cancer cannot live. This program is also good for curing arthritis and losing weight.

_____ 6. Hormone treatment. This treatment increases the hormones in your body that fight against the cancer. It must be taken for five months.

_____ 7. A diet consisting only of breads, cheeses, fats, and wine. This must be followed strictly for five months until your body is clean.

_____ 8. Surgery to take out the part of the body with cancer. This is followed by four months of treatments using special medicines to kill the cancer.

REVIEWING LANGUAGE

A. EXPLORING LANGUAGE

Read the following sentences. Then rewrite each sentence, but change the underlined word to a word from the list below. You may need to change the form of the word to be grammatically correct. The rest of the sentence should remain the same.

harmless	guarantee	founder	victim (of)	offer
specialize	arthritis	fraud	discovery	unproven

1. The quack <u>provided</u> testimonials for interested people to read.

_____

2. If you know someone who has <u>joints that are often sore</u>, tell that person to talk to Benjamin Harrison.

_____

3. Even though many people believe taking large amounts of vitamins can cure some diseases, this cure is <u>not definitely true</u>.

_____

4. The product came with a <u>paper that said it would definitely work</u>.

_____

5. The <u>thing that nobody had ever seen before</u> was a new medicine from the rain forest.

_____

6. Some telemarketers are <u>people who lie to you to make a profit</u>.

_____

7. "Quacks Anonymous" is an organization that helps victims of fraud. The <u>person who started it</u> is a successful businesswoman from California.

_____

8. Luis is a doctor who <u>has special knowledge</u> in medicine for children.

_____

9. The <u>person who was harmed by</u> health fraud called the National Council Against Health Fraud to report the quack.

_____

10. Many quack products are <u>not going to hurt anyone</u>.

_____

B. WORKING WITH WORDS

Work in pairs. First, Student A will write four questions using four of the words in the first column, and Student B will write four questions using four of the words in the second column. Underline the vocabulary word in each of the questions you write. Then, partners will exchange papers and write the answers to each other's questions using the underlined word. Discuss your answers with your partner.

Example

The word you have to use is _medicine_.
You write this question:

Have you ever taken a <u>medicine</u> that didn't come from a doctor?

Your partner writes his or her answer under the question and explains.

Student A	Student B
miracle	harmless
quack	fraud
offer	clinic
qualified	guarantee
unproven	victim
discovery	specialize

SKILLS FOR EXPRESSION

A. GRAMMAR: Adjectives—Superlatives

1 *Look at the following advertisement and notice the phrases that are underlined.*

New Formula Cures Baldness!

It's California's <u>best-kept secret</u>. Researchers have just found th<u>e most advanced cure</u> for baldness. HAIR THERE is its name. It's easy to use and makes your hair thicker instantly. Now, you can be <u>the most attractive</u> that you've ever been. And no one will ever know your secret. Finally there is a solution to the problem of losing hair.
HAIR THERE – <u>the most important hair product</u> you can buy!

Compare the following sentences. How are they different?

1. a. It's California's better kept secret.

   b. It's California's best-kept secret.

2. a. Researchers have just found a more advanced cure for baldness.

   b. Researchers have just found the most advanced cure for baldness.

3. a. Now, you can be a more attractive man.

   b. Now, you can be the most attractive man.

4. a. HAIR THERE—a more important hair product.

   b. HAIR THERE—the most important hair product.

Adjectives: Superlatives

FOCUS ON GRAMMAR

See Adjectives: Superlatives in *Focus on Grammar, Intermediate.*

We use the superlative form of the adjective when we are comparing two or more things, and when we want to emphasize that one of the things has an exceptional quality. Imagine, for example, that there are three baldness products on sale. One costs ten dollars, one costs fifteen dollars, and one costs twenty dollars. The ten-dollar product is **the least expensive** one. The twenty-dollar product is **the most expensive** one.

There are different ways to form the superlative.

a. For most one- or two-syllable adjectives ending in *-y*, use *the + adjective + -est.*

tall	the tallest
happy	the happiest
dark	the darkest
heavy	the heaviest

b. For most adjectives with two or more syllables, use *the most/the least +* **adjective.**

beautiful	the most beautiful
intelligent	the most intelligent

c. There are also some irregular superlative forms.

good	the best
bad	the worst
little	the least
far	the farthest/the furthest

2 *Look at the following testimonial for the Organic Health Center. Complete the sentences. Use the superlative form of the adjectives in parentheses. Don't forget to use **the**.*

Example: She is _____the smartest_____ person I've ever met.
                              (smart)

To whom it may concern:

In 1997, I was diagnosed with cancer. I went through the treatments the doctors ordered. The doctors promised me I was getting better. But I could tell that I wasn't. My health was _____
                                                                                 1. (bad)
it had ever been.

Then I heard of Benjamin Harrison's Organic Health Center. I talked with him and asked him many questions. After talking with Benjamin, I could tell that he was _____ of anyone I had talked to.
                              2. (educated)
It became clearer and clearer to me that using Western medicine was not

_____ way to take care of my cancer.
      3. (intelligent)
I decided to try Benjamin's cure for cancer. After only two weeks, I felt much better. And Benjamin's cure was _____
                                                            4. (easy)
treatment of all the ones I tried.

I would like everyone who reads this letter to know that I was cured after only three months. It has now been ten months, and my health is

_____ it's ever been. My doctors say that my recovery is
      5. (good)
_____ recovery they've ever seen. This is because Benjamin
      6. (fast)
is _____ health professional I know.
      7. (dedicated)

I want to thank Benjamin for being _____ person
                                                8. (helpful)
I met during my illness. Without his help, I might not be alive today! And, if you have cancer, contact Benjamin immediately. You deserve to

be _____ person you can be.
      9. (healthy)

                                        Sincerely,

                                        Cheryl B.

B. STYLE: Summary Writing

1 *Look at Reading Two, "The Organic Health Center." Then read the summary of "The Organic Health Center" below. The summary is written in the third person, while the original is written in the first person. How else are they different?*

SUMMARY OF "THE ORGANIC HEALTH CENTER"

"The Organic Health Center" is an advertisement for a clinic to cure cancer. The founder is Benjamin Harrison. Through his travels, Harrison learned the causes and the cure of cancer. As a result, he now offers a treatment that works on the whole body using a healthy diet. The clinic has several programs for different diseases, and they are all guaranteed.

A **summary** is a shorter version of a text. It helps the reader understand the most important information. There are several parts of a summary.

a. It contains the main idea or topic of the text.

b. It contains the important supporting details of the text. A supporting detail is a fact or example that helps explain the main idea.

c. It contains definitions of important words.

d. It doesn't contain any of the reader's opinions or any other information.

e. It is approximately one-fourth the length of the text.

2 *Work in a small group. Look at the sentences below. One sentence is the topic sentence for "A Miracle Cure?" It contains the main idea of the article. Each of the other sentences is an important supporting detail. First, identify the topic sentence. Label it **TS**. Then, identify the paragraph from Reading One in which each supporting detail appears. Put the sentences in the correct order. Label them **SD1, SD2**, etc. (Ignore the blanks in the sentences for now. You will fill them in later in the exercise.)*

_____ 1. People often go to quacks because they want an easy solution for their problem and because they are afraid.

_____ 2. Quacks _____ use similar techniques for selling their products.

_____ 3. Many people are using quacks instead of doctors.

_____ 4. It can be difficult to know if someone is a quack, but there are ways.

_____ 5. Quacks understand this. _____ they sell products for illnesses that have no cure, and people who are afraid of dying will pay any price for them.

_____ 6. If you are concerned about buying something from a quack, there are people and organizations that can help you.

_____ 7. _____ , these people often don't realize how dangerous it is to use a quack. It is dangerous because the product usually doesn't work. _____ , the patient can be getting worse during the treatment.

3 *Now write the topic sentence and the supporting-detail sentences on a separate piece of paper so that you have a summary for "A Miracle Cure?" Copy the blank spaces also.*

In summary writing, it is important to read your summary and edit it. One of the ways to do this is to add transitions to make it flow. Look at the transitions below. Each one will fit into one of the sentences above. Add them. Then compare your summary with that of another student.

as a result   so   also   unfortunately

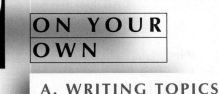

ON YOUR OWN

A. WRITING TOPICS

Choose one of the following topics. Write two or three paragraphs using some of the vocabulary, grammar, and style you learned in this unit.

a. Write your own fraudulent advertisement. Use pictures or illustrations to make it look like a real ad.

b. Most cultures have traditional treatments that have been used for many years. These treatments may not be scientific, but they seem to work. Explain how these treatments are both similar and different from quackeries.

c. Imagine that you have cancer. You have tried every medical treatment the doctors have recommended, and you are still getting worse. The doctors say they cannot help you anymore. Would you try a product or treatment that could be a quackery? Why or why not?

d. Do you think it is wrong for a quack to offer hope to someone who has been told he or she is dying? Why or why not?

B. FIELDWORK

Work in a small group to look at advertisements in magazines.
(Especially look at sports, fashion, and health magazines.) Start at the
back of the magazine since many ads are found there.

Step 1: Find one or two advertisements that you think may be
fraudulent and fill in the information below.

◆ Type of product or treatment: _____

◆ What the product is supposed to do: _____

◆ Reasons why this may be fraudulent:

a. _____

_____

b. _____

_____

c. _____

_____

d. _____

_____

e. _____

_____

◆ Do you think people will buy this product? Why or why
not? _____

◆ If your answer to the question above was yes, what kind of
person would buy this product?

_____

Step 2: Share your information with a small group of classmates.
Discuss what kinds of products seem to be popular with
quacks. Write a one-paragraph report summarizing your
group's findings.

THE METAMORPHOSIS

1 APPROACHING THE TOPIC

A. PREDICTING

Look at the photograph of the cockroach. Work in a small group.
Write as many adjectives as you can that describe the cockroach
and your feelings about cockroaches in general.

67

B. SHARING INFORMATION

Work in a small group. Discuss your answers to the following questions.

1. Have you ever had an insect fly into your ear, mouth, or eye or get into your clothes? How did you feel?

2. What kinds of insects are you afraid of? What kinds of insects do you like?

3. Have you ever had a bad dream about an insect? Explain.

4. Do you think insects are dirty? Why or why not?

5. Do you know of any insects that people like to eat?

6. Moviemakers have had success making movies about giant insects. Why do you think people like this type of movie?

2 PREPARING TO READ

A. BACKGROUND

1 *Read the following paragraph about Franz Kafka, the author of the story in Reading One.*

Franz Kafka was born in Prague (now in the Czech Republic) on July 3, 1883. He was the only son and had three younger sisters. His father was a very large, strong man with a powerful personality. His mother was more quiet. She was a thinker. Franz was like his mother. He was very small and skinny, and he had a weak personality. He was a thinker. He always felt that he was a disappointment to his father. Although he was engaged many times, he never got married. He died of tuberculosis at age forty.

grabbing, grabs

grab: to take quickly and roughly - to snatch

2 *Read the statements. Based on the text, do you agree or disagree? Discuss these statements with the class.*

1. Franz had a good relationship with his father. _NO_

2. Franz liked sports. _we don know_

3. He thought he would be a weak husband, so he never married.

4. He always compared himself to his father. _we don't know_

May be

B. VOCABULARY FOR COMPREHENSION

1 *Read the sentences. Try to guess the meaning of the underlined words. Write a definition or synonym on the line. Then compare your answers with the class. The first one has been done for you.*

a dramatic change from one stage of life to another

1. The <u>metamorphosis</u> of a caterpillar into a butterfly is an amazing thing. _A butterfly's change from cocoon to a winged insect._

   <u>change</u>

   contribute to

2. My parents <u>supported</u> me until I finished college, but then I had to get a job and pay for everything by myself.

   She supports her family by working two jobs.

   hisses

3. The <u>hiss</u> of a snake is a sound that would scare many people.

   The cat hissed at the dog

   The snake hissed at the mouth, then attacked it.

4. When she saw the spider, she <u>fainted</u> and fell down on the floor.

   I feel faint from the heat.

5. The thief <u>grabbed</u> the woman's purse and ran away with it.

   She grabbed the chance to work for the company

   To hit again and again

6. Someone was <u>beating</u> on the door, and the loud noise woke up everyone in the house.

   She beat the eggs with a spoon.

7. Some people don't want to get close to insects or touch them because they really don't like them. They think insects are <u>disgusting</u>. _= offensive_

   That garbage in the streets is disgusting.

hiss a low-pitched sound of air forced from the mouth

faint; to fall unconscious. unclear, weak.

What she says has substance because of her knowledge and experience.

8. Many smokers wish that they could remove the bad <u>substance</u> from cigarettes. Then they could smoke without worrying about their health.

meaning, truth

The substance in this container is toxic.

9. After the bee stung the child, he screamed and cried loudly. His mother held him in her arms and sang to him, and this finally <u>soothed</u> him enough to fall asleep.

She soothed the barking dog with a low, soft voice.

10. Firefighters are very <u>brave</u> when they go into burning buildings to save people.

_____

11. Some people enjoy a good, <u>smelly</u> cheese like blue cheese. Others don't like the bad smell and won't eat it.

_____

soothe
soothed
soothing
soothes
To ease mental or physical pain.
① *To calm and relax.*
②

2 *Now match the word with the correct synonym or phrase. Compare your answers with a partner.*

_____ 1. beat   a. take something quickly and roughly

_____ 2. disgusting   b. not be afraid of danger

_____ 3. faint   c. relieve

_____ 4. grab   d. a sound like a long *s*

_____ 5. hiss   e. anything one can touch

_____ 6. metamorphosis   f. hit repeatedly

_____ 7. brave   g. provide the money someone needs to live

_____ 8. smelly   h. something that is strongly disliked

_____ 9. soothe   i. something with a bad odor

_____ 10. substance   j. lose consciousness, as if you were asleep

_____ 11. support   k. a change from one form to another

3

READING ONE: The Metamorphosis

A. INTRODUCING THE TOPIC

The following paragraph is from the story you are going to read. As you read, think about the picture of the cockroach on page 67. Then answer the questions.

> *Well, it was time to get up. Surely, as soon as he got out of bed, he would realize this had all been a bad dream. He tried to move his back part out first, but it moved so slowly, and it was so difficult. His thin little legs seemed useless, just moving and moving in the air, not helping him at all. Then he tried the front part. This worked better, but he still couldn't move enough to get out of bed. He began rocking back and forth, stronger and stronger, and finally threw himself onto the floor, hitting his head as he fell.*

1. Something has happened to this man. Can you guess what it is?

   _____

   _____

2. What does this sentence mean: "Surely, as soon as he got out of bed, he would realize this had all been a bad dream?"

   _____

   _____

3. Why is it so hard for him to get out of bed?

   _____

   _____

4. What do you think the rest of the story will be about?

   _____

   _____

The following abridged story, "The Metamorphosis," was written by Franz Kafka (1883–1924).

The Metamorphosis

FRANZ KAFKA

1　One morning, Gregor Samsa woke up from a bad dream and realized he was some kind of terrible insect. He was a cockroach, and he was as large as a man! Lying on his back, he could see his large brown belly and thin legs. He tried to turn over onto his side, but every time he tried, he would roll onto his back again.

2　He began to think about his job as a traveling salesman. He hated his job, but he had to do it to support his father, mother, and sister because his father no longer worked. He looked at the clock and realized he had overslept—it was 6:30! He was late. The next train left at 7:00. He would have to hurry to make it. A few minutes later his mother yelled to him: "It's 6:45. You're late. Get up!" When he answered her, he was surprised to hear his voice; it sounded so high. "Yes, mother. I'm getting up now." His sister now whispered through the door, "Gregor, are you all right? Do you need anything?"

3　Well, it was time to get up. Surely, as soon as he got out of bed, he would realize this had all been a bad dream. He tried to move his back part out first, but it moved so slowly, and it was so difficult. His thin little legs seemed useless, just moving and moving in the air, not helping him at all. Then he tried the front part. This worked better, but he still couldn't move enough to get out of bed. He began rocking back and forth, stronger and stronger, and finally threw himself onto the floor, hitting his head as he fell.

4　All of a sudden, he heard a knock at the door. It was his manager, who had come to see why he was late. "Oh," thought Gregor, "I hate my job." Then the manager spoke. "Mr. Samsa, I must warn you that you could lose your job because of this. Lately, your work has not been very good, and now I find you in bed when you should be at work!" Gregor panicked and said, "No, no, I will come out immediately. I was sick, but now I feel much better." The manager and Gregor's family did not understand a single word he said, for his speech was now the hiss of an insect. As he talked, he managed to move himself to the chest of drawers, tried to stand up, then slipped and fell, holding tightly to a chair with his thin legs. He finally managed to open the door and lean against it.

5　At the sight of him, the manager screamed, his mother fainted, and his father wept. The manager began to back out of the room slowly, and Gregor realized he couldn't let him leave. He let go of the door and fell into the living room on his tiny little legs. Again his mother screamed, while the manager disappeared out the door. His father quickly grabbed a walking stick and a newspaper, and began beating Gregor back into his bedroom. Once Gregor was inside, the door was locked from the outside.

6　Gregor awoke as it was getting dark. He smelled food and saw that his sister, Grete, had left him one of his favorite meals, a bowl of milk with bread in it. But, when he tasted it, it tasted terrible, and he turned away in disgust. He slid under the couch and slept there until morning.

7　The next morning, Gregor's sister looked in and was surprised to see that he hadn't eaten a thing. She picked up the bowl and soon returned with some old vegetables, bones, and smelly cheese. After she left, Gregor hungrily ate them all up. And so the days passed, for she was the only one brave enough to come into the room.

8　Gregor grew tired of being in the bedroom day and night, and soon took to walking back and forth across the walls and ceiling. It felt much better than walking on the floor. His sister noticed this because of the brown sticky substance left from his feet wherever he walked. She decided to move most of the furniture out of the room so Gregor would have more walking space. But Gregor wanted to keep a picture on the wall—a picture of a beautiful woman dressed in pretty clothes. While Grete and her mother were in the other room, he quickly climbed the wall and pressed himself against the picture. When his mother saw him, she screamed and fainted. His sister then became very angry with him. He followed her into the dining room to help her, but this frightened her. When his father returned home and learned what had happened, he became very angry. Gregor tried to return to his bedroom, but couldn't fit through the doorway. Suddenly, his father started throwing apples at him. The first few didn't hurt him, but then one pierced his body, and he felt terrible pain. His mother ran to his father and begged him not to kill Gregor, as Gregor slowly crawled back to his room.

9　The apple remained in Gregor's back and stopped him from being able to walk easily. This gave him great pain. His sister also began to care less and less about feeding him and cleaning his room. Well, he wasn't very hungry anyway. The dust and dirt gradually became thick on the floor and stuck to him whenever he moved.

10　The family now left his door to the dining room open for two hours every night after dinner, and he could listen to their conversation. He really loved this. One night, they forgot to lock Gregor's door. When his sister began to play the violin, which she had not done for a long time, he felt so good. The music was beautiful and soothing. He had begun to walk toward her, thinking he would tell her how wonderful it was, when his family saw him. The music suddenly stopped. Grete became very upset. "Momma, Poppa," she said, "This cannot go on. We must find a way to get rid of this thing. It is destroying our lives."

11   Gregor slowly crawled back to his room. He lay there in the dark and couldn't move. Even the place in his back where the apple was no longer hurt. He thought of his family tenderly as he lay there, and, when the light began to come through the window, he died.

12   When Gregor was found dead the next morning, the whole family seemed to feel relieved. For the first time in a long, long time, they went out and took a train ride to the country, making plans for the future.

B. READING FOR MAIN IDEAS

Read the main ideas from the story. They are all false in some way. Rewrite each main idea so that it is correct.

1. Gregor dreams he has become an insect.

_____

_____

2. His family thinks it's funny when they see Gregor.

_____

_____

3. Only his mother takes care of him, and she continues to do this with great patience.

_____

_____

4. His father wants to get rid of him.

_____

_____

5. His family feels helpless.

_____

_____

6. He dies in the living room as he thinks of his job.

_____

_____

C. READING FOR DETAILS

To paraphrase a sentence means to say it in a different way, using your own words. The sentences below are paraphrases of sentences in the story. Find the sentence in the story that has the same meaning as each of the sentences below. The first one has been done for you.

1. His sister wanted to know if he was OK.

   His sister now whispered through the door, "Gregor, are you all right? Do you need anything?"

2. Even though it was better, he wasn't able to get up.

   _____

3. Because he was very afraid, he promised to quickly come out of his room.

   _____

4. The manager felt afraid and tried to leave carefully, and Gregor knew he must stop him.

   _____

5. He moved easily and quietly under the sofa and stayed there until the next day.

   _____

6. His sister was amazed early the next day when she noticed he had not touched his food.

   _____

7. At first they didn't hurt him, but then one cut into him and hurt him badly.

   _____

8. Gradually, his sister lost interest in taking care of him.

   _____

9. It's time to think of how to remove him.

   _____

10. He rested in the darkness without moving.

   _____

D. READING BETWEEN THE LINES

Answer the questions. Compare your answers with those of your classmates.

1. Did the story turn out the way you expected it to? Look back at your ideas about the story on page 71. Compare your predictions with the story.

   _____

   _____

   _____

2. Do you think this is a funny story? a sad story? a happy story? Explain.

   <u>a sad story</u>

   _____

   _____

3. Why do you think Kafka chose to have Gregor turn into a cockroach? Why not an animal?

   <u>I think Kafka shose a human</u>
   <u>because the human make</u>
   <u>more interstingly the story.</u>

4. What kind of relationship does Gregor have with his family? How does that affect Gregor's feelings about himself?

   <u>No good. He hate his job,</u>
   <u>He must be supported by</u>
   <u>his family</u>

5. What is your opinion of Gregor at the end of the story? Do you see him the same way his family does?

   <u>The fami</u>

   _____

   _____

READING TWO: Ungeziefer

A. EXPANDING THE TOPIC

1 *Many critics have studied Kafka's stories. Read the following explanations of why Kafka wrote "The Metamorphosis" and what he was trying to show us in this story.*

Ungeziefer

1   "The Metamorphosis" is a short story which is both funny and sad at the same time. It is funny because of how Gregor must learn to move his new "cockroach" legs and body. On the other hand, it is sad because he loses the love of his family as a result of his becoming so disgusting.

2   Why did Kafka choose to tell a story about a man who turns into a cockroach? Certainly many people are afraid of cockroaches and other insects. They think cockroaches are ugly and disgusting. Why would Kafka choose something that most of us hate? What was his purpose?

3   Many critics[1] have written their ideas about Kafka's purpose. One explanation comes from a word that Kafka used in his story. Kafka wrote his story in German, and he used the German word *ungeziefer,* or *vermin*, which can be used to mean a person who is rough and disgusting. In English, we do the same thing. If we call a person a "cockroach," we mean that the person is weak and cowardly.[2] Gregor, the man, is like a cockroach. He is weak and disgusting. Why? Because he doesn't want to be the supporter of his family. He hates his job and wishes he didn't have to do it in order to pay off the family debt.[3] In addition, his family has been like a parasite to him. Gregor's family have all enjoyed relaxing, not working, while he alone has had to work. When he becomes a cockroach, he becomes the parasite[4] to the family. So Gregor's true self is metamorphosed

---

[1] *critic:* a person who gives opinions about the quality of something, especially art, literature, music, etc.
[2] *cowardly:* weak and afraid, easily frightened
[3] *debt:* money that you owe to someone
[4] *parasite:* an animal or plant that lives in or on another animal or plant and gets its food from it

into an insect because his true self wants to be like a child again, helpless and having no responsibility.

4   Another explanation comes from Kafka's relationship with his father. Kafka was a small, quiet man. He saw himself as weak and spineless compared to his father, who was physically large and had a powerful personality. It is the same with Gregor. He also sees himself as a failure. By turning himself into an insect, Gregor is able to rebel against his father, and, at the same time, punish himself for rebelling. This punishment results in his being physically and emotionally separated from his family with no hope of joining them again, and finally he dies.

5   Kafka's choice of an insect makes this story work because many people feel insects are disgusting. Gregor becomes the vermin, the disgusting son that nobody cares about. His family rejects him because of his appearance, yet he continues to love them to the end.

2 *Write answers to the questions below on a separate piece of paper.*

1. Do the critics think this is a funny story, a sad story, or a happy story? Why?

2. Why do the critics think Kafka chose to have Gregor turn into a cockroach, not an animal?

3. What kind of relationship do the critics think Gregor had with his family and how did that affect his feelings about himself?

4. What is the critics' opinion of Gregor at the end of the story?

B. LINKING READINGS ONE AND TWO

Now, compare the critics' ideas with your ideas in Section 3D. Was your interpretation more or less critical of Gregor than the critics'? Then compare your answers above with those of your classmates. Which answers are similar? Which are different?

REVIEWING LANGUAGE

A. EXPLORING VOCABULARY

Discuss the following questions with a partner. Try to use the underlined words in your answers.

1. What insects or other living things do you know that make a <u>hissing</u> noise?

2. You may have seen the <u>metamorphosis</u> of a caterpillar into a butterfly. A caterpillar becomes a butterfly. What do the insects in Column A become? Match them with the correct item in Column B.

Column A	**Column B**
_____ 1. Maggot	a. Butterfly
_____ 2. Caterpillar	b. Beetle
_____ 3. Grub	c. Fly
_____ 4. Caterpillar	d. Moth

a.

b.

c.

d.

Stages of Metamorphosis

suits me (fit me)

3. In your culture, how long do parents usually <u>support</u> their children? Until they finish high school? college? get married? buy a house?

4. What insects do you think are <u>disgusting</u>? Why?

5. Try to think of what the following <u>substances</u> are made of:

   paper   blood   soap

6. Think of a person whom you think is <u>brave</u>. Explain.

7. Have you ever <u>fainted</u> or seen someone else <u>faint</u>? Explain.

8. When you are tired or worried about something, what <u>soothes</u>, or relieves, you?

9. What musical instruments produce sound when they are <u>beaten</u>?

B. WORKING WITH WORDS

We often use past-tense verbs when we are telling a story. There are several past-tense verbs in "The Metamorphosis." The past tense of the verb is usually formed by adding -ed to the base form of the verb. For example, *walk* becomes *walked, like* becomes *liked,* etc. However, there are many verbs which don't follow this pattern. For example, *sleep* becomes *slept, know* becomes *knew,* and *teach* becomes *taught.* These are called "irregular" verbs.

1 *Look at Reading One again. Underline all the regular past tense verbs and circle all the irregular past tense verbs. Remember that you must know the base form of the verb if you want to find it in the dictionary.*

2 *Write the irregular past tense forms for the verbs on page 81. You will find them in the paragraphs indicated. The first one has been done for you.*

	Paragraph	Simple Present Tense	Irregular Past Tense
a.	2	begin	began
b.	3 & 4	fall	*fell*
c.	5	weep	*wept*
d.	6	awake	*awoke*
e.	6	sleep	*slept*
f.	8	feel	*felt*
g.	9	stick	*stuck*
h.	10	forget	*forgot*
i.	11	think	*thought*
j.	12	find	*found*
k.	12	take	*took*

6 SKILLS FOR EXPRESSION

A. GRAMMAR: Infinitives of Purpose

1 *Look at the following sentences taken from the text and notice the part that is underlined.*

- ◆ He followed her into the dining room <u>to help</u> her.
- ◆ Why did he follow her into the dining room? <u>To help</u> her.

Read the following sentences. Underline the verbs that have the form to + verb. What questions do these verbs answer?

a. Gregor worked to support his family.

b. His sister whispered to him to ask if he was all right.

c. He rocked back and forth to get out of bed.

Look at the questions and answers below.

Question about Action	**Purpose**
Why did Gregor work?	He wanted **to support** his family.
Why did his sister whisper to him?	She wanted **to ask** if he was all right.
Why did he rock back and forth?	He wanted **to get out** of bed.

Now we can combine the questions and answers to make the original sentences.

◆ Gregor worked **to support** his family.

◆ His sister whispered to him **to ask** if he was all right.

◆ He rocked back and forth **to get out** of bed.

FOCUS ON GRAMMAR

See Infinitives of Purpose in *Focus on Grammar, Intermediate.*

Infinitives of Purpose

Infinitives that are used to explain the purpose of an action are called **infinitives of purpose.** They answer the question "Why?"

You can also use the longer form *in order to* **+ verb**.

◆ Gregor worked **in order to support** his family.

◆ His sister whispered to him **in order to ask** if he was all right.

2 *Match the question on the left with the answer on the right. The first one has been done for you.*

Question about Action

___d___ 1. Why did Gregor's manager come to his house?

_____ 2. Why was Gregor locked in his room?

_____ 3. Why did his father grab a walking stick and newspaper?

_____ 4. Why did Grete go into Gregor's room every day?

_____ 5. Why did Gregor follow Grete into the dining room?

_____ 6. Why did Gregor come out of his room?

_____ 7. Why did his family take a train ride?

Purpose

a. She needed to feed him.

b. He wanted to listen to the music.

c. He wanted to help her.

d. He wanted to see why Gregor was late.

e. They wanted to celebrate his death.

f. His family wanted to keep him there.

g. He wanted to beat Gregor.

3 *Now combine the questions and answers to make sentences that answer the question* **Why?**

1. Gregor's manager came to his house to see why he was late.

2. _____

3. _____

4. _____

5. _____

6. _____

7. _____

B. STYLE: Paraphrasing

1 *Look back to the exercise in Section 3C. Find the word or words in each paraphrased sentence that mean the same thing as the words below.*

Word(s) in Original Sentence	Word(s) in Paraphrased Sentence
1. all right	OK
2. to get out of bed	
3. come out immediately	
4. realized	
5. couch	
6. surprised	
7. pierced his body	
8. feeding him and cleaning his room	
9. to get rid of	
10. dark	

To **paraphrase** a sentence means to say it in a different way, using your own words. The meaning of the original sentence doesn't change, but the words do. You can paraphrase sentences by using synonyms or by wording phrases differently. Look at the following sentences from the reading and notice how they have been changed.

Original:	I **hate** my job.
Paraphrase:	I **don't like** my job.
Original:	It was his **manager**, who had come **to see** why he was late.
Paraphrase:	It was his **boss**, who had come **to find out** why he was late.
Original:	**Lately**, your work has **not been very good**.
Paraphrase:	**Recently**, your work has **been bad**.

2 *Paraphrase the sentences below. Replace the underlined word or words in the original sentence with a synonym or phrase that has the same meaning.*

1. I was sick, but now I feel <u>much better</u>.

   I was sick, but now I feel fine.

2. Again his mother screamed, while the manager <u>disappeared out the door</u>.

   again

3. But, when he <u>tasted</u> it, it tasted <u>terrible</u>, and he turned away in disgust.

4. She was the only one brave enough <u>to come into</u> the room.

5. This cannot <u>go on</u>.

3 *Paraphrase the sentences below. You can replace any of the words or phrases. Make sure that your paraphrase has the same meaning as the original sentence.*

1. Yes, Mother. I'm getting up now.

2. His father no longer worked.

3. The manager and Gregor's family did not understand a single word he said.

   nothing he said made sense to them.

4. Someone was beating on the door.

   Someone was thump on the door

5. Some people think insects are disgusting.

   Some people think insects are

   repulsive

   repugnant   offensive

People commonly consider the insect repulsive

People commonly consider the insect are repulsive

7 ON YOUR OWN

A. WRITING TOPICS

Choose one of the following topics. Write two or three paragraphs, using some of the vocabulary, grammar, and style you learned in this unit.

a. Choose a short story from your home country and write it in English. Find one that uses insects or animals if you can.

b. Use your imagination to write your own short story. Write a story that uses insects or animals if you can.

c. Explain your reaction to "The Metamorphosis." Did you like the story or not? Why? Which character in the story did you like the best? the least?

B. FIELDWORK

Step 1: Go to the library or a local bookstore and find a short story about an animal or insect to read.

Step 2: Draw or paint a large illustration of the story.

Step 3: Give an oral presentation about the story you chose. You might like to explain the title, say what country the story comes from, and then tell the story.

SPEAKING OF GENDER . . .

1 APPROACHING THE TOPIC

A. PREDICTING

Look at the photograph. Read the title of the unit. Take five minutes to describe the photograph in writing. Do you think the baby is a boy or a girl? Why? Share your answer with the class.

B. SHARING INFORMATION

*Often boys and girls are given different types of toys, games, and clothing. Fill in the chart below about your home culture. First, under the **Boys** column, list a toy that only boys play with. Then, under the **Girls** column, list a toy that only girls play with. In the last column, write a toy that both boys and girls play with. Do the same for games and clothing. Share your chart with another student and then with the class.*

Example

Your home culture: The United States

	Boys	Girls	Both
Toys	Truck	Doll	Kite

Your home culture: _____

	Boys	Girls	Both
Toys			
Games			
Clothing			

2 PREPARING TO READ

A. BACKGROUND

1 *Nowadays, many couples have a sonogram, or picture, taken of their unborn baby. Sonograms make it possible to see if the baby has any health problems. Many times you can also see the sex of the baby. Without sonograms, people still try to guess the sex of a baby before it is born. What are some of the ways people try to guess the sex of a baby in your home culture? Work in a small group. Write as many ways as you can think of. Share your list with another group. Are any of the ways similar? Which ones?*

_____

_____

_____

_____

_____

_____

_____

_____

_____

2 *Read each of the following statements. If you agree, write* **A.** *If you disagree, write* **D.** *When you are finished, compare your answers with those of another student.*

_____ **1.** Boys and girls are treated differently even before they are born.

_____ **2.** From birth, a child knows how to behave as a male or female.

_____ **3.** In my culture, it's better to be a boy.

_____ **4.** In my culture, it's better to be a girl.

B. VOCABULARY FOR COMPREHENSION

Read the sentences. Cross out one of the words below each sentence that doesn't fit the context of the sentence. The first one has been done for you.

1. Even though Sara is only six years old, she is already so <u>feminine</u>. Her dress and her hair are so soft and pretty. She is so polite, carefully saying "please" and "thank you" at just the right time.

   a. girlish   **b.** ladylike   **c.** ~~proud~~

2. In North American culture, most people think a cowboy is very <u>masculine</u>. He has male characteristics, such as strength and courage.

   a. soft   **b.** tough   **c.** bold

3. For most people, their gender is an important part of who they are (or how they act). It is an important part of their <u>identity</u>.

   a. self   **b.** wealth   **c.** role

4. Language <u>reflects</u> the culture of the people that speak it. You can't understand a people's language if you don't understand their culture.

   a. shows   **b.** expresses   **c.** shines on

5. The children <u>competed</u> in a contest. They wanted to see who could jump rope the most times in a row and not miss.

   a. tried to win   **b.** tried to be the best   **c.** tried to help each other

6. When a boy is playing with a ball and will not give it to his sister, she might say "You're not playing <u>fairly</u>. Play fair. It's my turn."

   a. with tricks   **b.** by sharing equally   **c.** by the rules

7. Parents <u>influence</u> the way their children think and act. Children learn a lot from them.

   a. guide   **b.** ignore   **c.** change

8. American culture <u>emphasizes</u> success for men and beauty for women.

   a. makes confused   **b.** makes important   **c.** gives value to

9. In American culture, a man gains <u>status</u> by marrying a beautiful woman, and a woman gains <u>status</u> by marrying a successful man.

    a. trouble in society   **b.** power in society   **c.** importance in society

10. People sometimes like to <u>gossip</u> about other people.

    a. talk about secrets   **b.** talk about behavior   **c.** talk about health

11. In some cultures, having many children <u>proves</u> a man is masculine.

    a. shows clearly   **b.** shows frequently   **c.** shows to be true

READING ONE: Different Ways of Talking

A. INTRODUCING THE TOPIC

Read the first paragraph of the text. Then write your answers to the following questions.

1. How did Joy's parents respond to the news that they were having a girl? What did they do?

2. What did their friends and relatives do? What other things could they have done?

3. What do you think the reading will be about?

_____

_____

_____

_____

_____

_____

_____

_____

Discuss your ideas with the class. Then continue reading "Different Ways of Talking."

Different Ways of Talking

1   A few hours after Joy Fisher's birth, her parents took pictures of her. Joy's mother put a pink hairband around Joy's head, so that everyone who saw the pictures would know that the new baby was a girl. Even before she was born, Joy's parents knew that she was going to be female. Joy's mother had a sonogram when she was six months pregnant. When the doctor said, "I'm sure you have a little lady in there," Joy's parents told all their relatives and friends that their baby was a girl. Gifts soon arrived, including pink dresses and dolls. Joy's parents decorated her room in pink and white.

2   A few years later, Joy's brother, Tommy, was born. His room was painted blue, and he received books and a football as gifts. Joy enjoyed helping her mother take care of the new baby. She also enjoyed playing with other girls at school. Now, Tommy has also entered school, where he plays with other boys. The games Joy and Tommy play are quite different. Joy loves jumping rope with her two best friends. Tommy likes to play ball with a large group of boys. Sometimes when they play a game, he is the captain. He enjoys telling the other boys what to do. Joy, on the other hand, doesn't like it when new girls join her friends and try to change the way they jump rope. She thinks that some of these girls are too bossy.

3   Both Joy and Tommy are growing up in the culture of the United States. They are learning what it means to be a girl and a boy in this culture. Their sex at birth, female and male, is now becoming a gender—a way of thinking, speaking, and acting that is considered feminine or masculine. Each culture has its own way of defining gender, and very early in life gender becomes a basic part of a person's identity. According to Deborah Tannen, a professor at Georgetown University, gender differences are even reflected in the ways that men and women use language. Tannen and others who study communication believe that these differences begin early in life.

4   For example, in the United States, boys and girls usually play in same-sex groups. Boys might play in large groups in which every boy knows his place. Some are leaders; others are followers. Boys compete with one another for leadership. Many boys like to get attention by boasting, or talking about how well they can do things. The games that they play often have complicated rules, and each boy tries hard to win.

5   Girls, in contrast, usually play in smaller groups. Sometimes they play with only one or two "best friends." Most girls want other girls to like them, and this is more important to them than winning. Girls may be interested in playing fairly and taking turns. For example, when girls jump rope together, two girls hold the rope while others jump. Then the rope-holders take their turn jumping.

6   Tannen has found that these differences are reflected in the ways that children use language while they play. Boys often use commands when they talk to each other. For instance, when Tommy is captain he might say, "You go first. Don't wait for me." As the leader of the other boys, he tells them exactly what to do. But when Joy wants to influence her friends, she uses different forms of language. Instead of using commands, she will say, "Let's try it this way. Let's do this." This is how she tries to direct the other girls without sounding bossy. By using the form "let's," she also emphasizes the fact that the girls all belong to the same group.

7   As Joy and Tommy grow up, they will continue to speak differently. In junior high school, Joy's status will depend on her circle of friends. If her friends are popular, then Joy may enjoy high status at school. For this reason, Joy and many other girls are interested in gossip. If Joy has some information to share about a popular girl at school, this proves that she has a friendship with this girl. In this way Joy can use gossip to gain more status in her school.

8   Tommy, on the other hand, may be less interested in gossip. His status does not depend on who his friends are at school. Tommy gains status through his own ability to play sports well or earn high grades. Later in life, Joy may continue to be interested in talking about other people and their lives. Tommy will be less interested in personal talk and more concerned with discussions of sports and news. These give him a chance to gain status by showing others his knowledge.

9   Different ways of speaking are part of gender. As adults, men and women sometimes face difficulties in their communication with each other. Studies of communication show that if a woman tells her husband about a problem, she will expect him to listen and offer sympathy. She may be annoyed when he simply tells her how to solve the problem. Similarly, a husband may be annoyed when his wife wants to stop and ask a stranger for directions to a park or restaurant. Unlike his wife, he would rather use a map and find his way by himself.

10   Language is also part of the different ways that men and women think about friendship. Most American men believe that friendship means doing things together such as camping or playing tennis. Talking is not an important part of friendship for most of them. American women, on the other hand, usually identify their best friend as someone with whom they talk frequently. Tannen believes that for women, talking with friends and agreeing with them is very important. Tannen has found that women, in contrast to men, often use tag questions. For example, a woman might say, "This is a great restaurant, isn't it?" By adding a tag question to her speech ("isn't it?"), she is giving other people a chance to agree with her. Unlike most women, men often speak more directly, giving direct commands such as "Close the door." Many women, however, use more polite forms such as "Could you please close the door?"

11   These differences seem to be part of growing up in the United States' culture and following its rules of gender. If men and women can understand that many of their differences are cultural, not personal, they may be able to improve their relationships. They may begin to understand that because of gender differences in language, there is more than one way to communicate.

Did the reading include the information you expected? Look back at your list of ideas on page 91.

B. READING FOR MAIN IDEAS

*Read each statement and decide if it is true or false. Write **T** or **F**. If a statement is false, rewrite it to make it true. The first one has been done for you.*

Gender
__F__ **1.** A child's sex at birth determines how the child will think, act, and speak later in life.

_____ **2.** People learn masculine and feminine behavior.

_____ **3.** Men and women learn to use language differently.

_____ **4.** Gender differences can be seen in the ways that children use language when they fight.

_____ **5.** Differences in language between males and females are the same in all cultures.

_____ **6.** Girls gain status by showing their knowledge about sports and news.

_____ **7.** Girls get much of their identity from being part of a group.

_____ **8.** Men usually talk more about other people than women do.

_____ **9.** For women, talking with friends is an important part of friendship.

_____ **10.** Sex is biological and gender is cultural.

C. READING FOR DETAILS

Read the following questions. Choose the best answer. Write the number of the paragraph where you found the answer. The first one has been done for you.

Paragraph

1. In what kind of group does Tommy like to play?   __2__

   a. He likes to play in groups of both boys and girls.

   b. He likes to play in large groups.

   c. He likes to play in small groups.

Paragraph

2. How did Joy's mother first show that Joy was a girl?   _____
   a. She put a hairband around her head.
   b. She put a pink dress on her.
   c. She painted her room blue.

3. What does Tommy like about being captain?   _____
   a. He likes boasting.
   b. He likes telling other boys what to do.
   c. He likes having the other boys like him.

4. How do boys get attention?   _____
   a. They argue with others.
   b. They talk about their abilities.
   c. They change the rules.

5. Who do girls usually play with?   _____
   a. They play with small groups of girls.
   b. They play with large groups of girls.
   c. They play with groups of both boys and girls.

6. What is one reason why girls are interested in gossip?   _____
   a. Gossip teaches them how to act.
   b. Gossip allows them to use commands.
   c. Gossip can bring them status.

7. Why might a woman get angry with her husband?   _____
   a. She feels that he doesn't listen.
   b. She feels that his advice is wrong.
   c. She feels that he doesn't care.

8. How do American men show friendship?   _____
   a. They show friendship by talking together often.
   b. They show friendship by agreeing with each other.
   c. They show friendship by doing things together.

Paragraph

9. Why do women often use tag questions?　　　＿＿＿＿＿

    a. They want to speak directly.

    b. They want to be polite.

    c. They want to give others a chance to agree with them.

10. If people learn more about different ways of communication, . . .　　　＿＿＿＿＿

    a. they will speak more directly.

    b. they can have better relationships.

    c. they might understand children better.

D. READING BETWEEN THE LINES

Look at Reading One to find information to help you answer the questions below. Which is the most likely answer, in your opinion? Put the number of the paragraph where you found your answer in the blank on the right. Then discuss your answers. (More than one answer may be possible for some questions.)

Paragraph

1. When do gender differences between boys and girls begin?　　　＿＿＿＿＿

    a. before birth

    b. at birth

    c. shortly after birth

2. Why were different colors used in the children's rooms?　　　＿＿＿＿＿

    a. for variety

    b. because of preference

    c. as a reflection of gender

Paragraph

3. What might Tommy do if he played with Joy and
   her friends?   _____

   a. argue with them

   b. tell them what to do

   c. invite other boys to join the group

4. Compared to Tommy's friendships, Joy's friendships
   are probably . . .   _____

   a. more boring.

   b. longer lasting.

   c. less competitive.

5. "Gender" refers to behavior that is considered
   masculine or feminine according to . . .   _____

   a. each person.

   b. members of a culture.

   c. family members.

6. Which of the following is emphasized in girls' speech? _____

   a. belonging to a group

   b. playing fairly

   c. being liked

7. What do some men want to prove by
   discussing sports?   _____

   a. They are knowledgeable.

   b. They are masculine.

   c. They are interested in sports.

8. What do the differences in male and female
   language show?   _____

   a. Human relationships are difficult.

   b. Human communication is not simple.

   c. Humans can be divided into two genders.

READING TWO: Speaking of Gender...

A. EXPANDING THE TOPIC

1 *Read the following interview. Dr. Glib Speakwell is a professor of communications at a well-known university. She is being interviewed by Gigi Jones, a reporter for Lingo Magazine.*

Lingo Magazine

Speaking of Gender...

Gigi Jones (GJ): I know you've written a lot about gender and language, Dr. Speakwell.

Dr. Speakwell (DS): Yes, I have. I find it very interesting. For example, you just called me "Doctor." That used to always suggest a man, not a woman.

GJ: Maybe I should call you "Doctorette."

DS: Actually, I prefer to be called "Doctor."

GJ: Why is that?

DS: Well, you know, English has several feminine words that people sometimes use when they're referring to women. You probably know them, right. What do you call a female poet?

GJ: A poetess?

DS: Yes, and a singer is a songstress, and a bachelor is . . .

GJ: A bachelorette?

DS: Yes. A bachelorette. Now these words aren't used too often, but they exist in the language. However, some women don't like such words because they feel . . . well, frankly, they feel as if these words make them less important than men.

GJ: What do you mean by that?

DS: For instance, if you say the word "actress," people don't always think of a serious artist. They might think of some silly, beautiful female who's more worried about her makeup than she is about Shakespeare. But when you say "actor" —that's not silly at all. That's a serious word, a respectable word.

GJ: I see.

DS: That's why I would never call myself a doctorette. Or a professoress—never!

GJ: Fine. I'll call you doctor.

DS: And what about you? Should I call you Miss Jones? Mrs. Jones?

GJ: Ms. Jones, please.

DS: Exactly—*Ms.* Jones. That's a very good example of how the language has changed in recent years, partly as a result of the women's movement.

GJ: You mean the title of *Ms.*?

DS: Not just that. We've changed dozens of words related to occupations. Think of all the words that used to end in -*man. Policeman, fireman, mailman, . . .*

GJ: I guess they've all changed. Now we say *police officer, firefighter, . . .* but what about *mailman*?

DS: *Mail carrier.* And do you know why? We've removed gender from these words because, after all, both men and women can do these jobs.

GJ: I suppose. But not everyone would agree with you.

DS: Maybe not. But you know, even though I believe men and women are equal in their abilities, I do think there are differences in the way they speak.

GJ: Do you really think so?

DS: Absolutely. Look at all the color words that women know! If a man and woman go shopping together, the man will look at a shirt and say, *I like the purple one.* But a woman will look at the same shirt and call it *lavender* . . . or *periwinkle.* . . .

GJ: Or *mauve?*

DS: Right! Women use more words for color. They also use some adjectives that men don't use . . . such as *lovely, cute, adorable.*

GJ: I guess you're right. Most men don't seem to use those words.

DS: Most of them don't. But you know, language and gender are both so closely related to culture. If you travel to other cultures, you'll find all sorts of amazing things.

GJ: Isn't that the topic of your newest book?

DS: Yes. I studied seventeen countries, and I found out that in Japan, for example, men and women use different word endings. So if a man doesn't want to sound bossy, he'll use the feminine word ending, -*no*, instead of -*ka. Ka* sounds more masculine, more direct.

GJ: So a man will talk like a woman in certain situations. Fascinating. What other interesting behaviors are there?

DS: It all depends on the culture. The Zulus in Africa have an interesting rule. If you're a woman, you're not allowed to say the name of your father-in-law.

GJ: That's new to me. But I've heard of people here who won't talk to their mothers-in-law.

DS: So have I. That will be the topic of my next book!

2 *Discuss these questions with the class.*

1. Do you agree with Dr. Speakwell's idea that men and women speak differently? Give examples to support your opinion.

2. In English, there are three titles for women: *Miss, Mrs.,* and *Ms.* How are they different? Why do you think *Ms.* is used today? What titles are used in your native language for men or women?

3. In your opinion, do men or women have higher status in Zulu society? Explain.

4. At the end of the interview, Gigi Jones makes a joke about mothers-in-law. Can you explain the meaning of this joke? Why do you think there are people who won't speak to their mothers-in law?

B. LINKING READINGS ONE AND TWO

Write the answers to these questions. Then discuss them with the class.

1. Compare English and your native language or another language you know well:

   ◆ Are there masculine and feminine word forms, such as *actor/actress*?

   ◆ Are there different word endings men and women are required to use?

   ◆ Are there any words men or women are not permitted to say?

2. How are Dr. Speakwell's ideas and Deborah Tannen's ideas alike? For example, in paragraph 3 of Reading One, we read that Tannen believes that differences in gender can be seen in how men and women use language. In Reading Two, Dr. Speakwell agrees with Tannen: "But you know, even though I believe men and women are equal in their abilities, I do think there are differences in the way they speak." Can you find more examples of how their ideas are alike?

3. Imagine that you are a reporter. In the space below, write a question for Dr. Speakwell. Share your question with another student, and discuss possible answers.

_____

_____

_____

REVIEWING LANGUAGE

A. EXPLORING LANGUAGE

Read the quotations and decide whether each is more usual for a male or female to say. Write M or F. Use the readings to help you decide. Explain your answer to the class, using information from the readings.

_____ 1. "Let's try it again."

_____ 2. "Don't throw it to him!"

_____ 3. "Look at me. I can jump higher than you."

_____ 4. "It's a beautiful day, isn't it?"

_____ 5. "You're my best friend."

_____ 6. "Did you see the game last night?"

_____ 7. "Excuse me. Can you tell me where Chestnut Street is?"

_____ 8. "Give me the book."

_____ 9. "I don't think they're going to win this year."

_____ 10. "What a lovely gift. Thank you."

_____ 11. "That's terrible. You poor thing."

_____ 12. "I'm trying to decide between a burgundy sweater and a rose one."

B. WORKING WITH WORDS

Look at the summary of Reading One below. Fill in the blanks with one of the following words. First, make sure that the word really fits into the meaning of the whole sentence. Then make sure that it fits into the sentence grammatically. (You may need to change the form of the word to do this.) Use each word only once.

feminine	masculine	emphasize	compete
fair	reflect	influence	gender
prove	status		

Boys and girls learn different ways of behaving, talking, and thinking. These different behaviors reflect differences in (**1**) _____ . In the American culture, boys learn to (**2**) _____ with each other in games, trying very hard to win and boasting about how well they can do things. These behaviors are considered (**3**) _____ . People expect boys to act in these ways. On the other hand, girls learn to be (**4**) _____ . They would rather have their friends like them than compete with them to win a game. Girls are more interested in being (**5**) _____ , or equal, when they play. As children grow up, their gender will (**6**) _____ their behavior. Language (**7**) _____ the gender of children. Boys usually give commands, while girls often make suggestions. When boys use commands, it (**8**) _____ their leadership. As they grow older, their (**9**) _____ in society will depend on different things. Boys will gain respect by their achievements in school and in sports, by their leadership, and by showing their knowledge. Girls will gain respect by having friends who are popular. Sharing gossip about a friend is one of the ways they (**10**) _____ their friendship.

SKILLS FOR EXPRESSION

A. GRAMMAR: Using Modals for Requests

1 *Read the passage from "Different Ways of Talking." Then read the following pairs of sentences. Which ones seem more polite? Circle your choice.*

Unlike most women, men often speak more directly, giving direct commands such as "Close the door." Many women, on the other hand, use polite forms such as "Could you please close the door?"

1. **a.** Would you answer the phone?

   b. Answer the phone.

2. **a.** Can you close the door?

   b. Close the door.

3. **a.** Bring some food to the party, OK?

   b. Would you mind bringing food to the party?

FOCUS ON GRAMMAR

See Modals for Requests in *Focus on Grammar, Intermediate.*

Modals for Requests

Can, could, and *would* are **modals.** They are often used to make polite requests.

Help me. ——————▶ **Can** you help me?

——————▶ **Could** you help me?

——————▶ **Would** you help me?

A related form is *would you mind* + **gerund.**

Help me. ——————▶ **Would you mind helping** me?

2 *Change the following sentences to polite requests.*

1. Speak up—I can't hear you.

   Could _____ ?

2. Repeat that one more time.

   Can _____ ?

3. Tell me what you mean.

   Can _____ ?

4. Say that again.

   Could _____ ?

5. Speak more slowly.

   Would you mind _____ ?

3 *Write a polite request for each situation below.*

1. You want to know which team won the basketball game last night.

   _____

   _____

   _____

2. You want someone to play on your team.

   _____

   _____

   _____

3. You want your friend to go shopping with you for a baby gift.

   _____

   _____

   _____

4. You want your friend to help you with your homework.

   _____

   _____

   _____

5. You want someone to give you directions to the library.

   _____

   _____

   _____

B. STYLE: Comparing and Contrasting

1 *Read the following paragraphs. Look at the underlined words. What do they mean?*

Different ways of speaking are part of gender. As adults, men and women sometimes face difficulties in their communication with each other. Studies of communication show that if a woman tells her husband about a problem, she will expect him to listen and offer sympathy. She may be annoyed when he simply tells her how to solve the problem. <u>Similarly</u>, a husband may be annoyed when his wife wants to stop and ask a stranger for directions to a park or restaurant. <u>Unlike</u> his wife, he would rather use a map and find his way by himself.

Language is <u>also</u> part of the different ways that men and women think about friendship. Most American men believe that friendship means doing things together such as camping or playing tennis. Talking is not an important part of friendship for most of them. American women, <u>on the other hand</u>, usually identify their best friend as someone with whom they talk frequently. Tannen believes that for women, talking with friends and agreeing with them is very important. Tannen has found that women, <u>in contrast</u> to men, often use tag questions. For example, a woman might say, "This is a great restaurant, isn't it?" By adding a tag question to her speech ("isn't it?"), she is giving other people a chance to agree with her. <u>Unlike</u> most women, men often speak more directly, giving direct commands such as "Close the door." Many women, <u>however</u>, use more polite forms such as "Could you please close the door?"

Transitions

Writers use **transitions** to help readers move from one idea to another. These words or phrases prepare the reader for what type of information will come next. A variety of transitions are used to compare, or show similarities, and to contrast, or show differences.

TRANSITIONS USED TO COMPARE

likewise   *similarly*   *also*

Friendship is important to women.

+ **Likewise**, it is important to men.

+ It is **also** important to men.

+ **Similarly**, it is important to men.

All of these sentences mean:

*Friendship is **important** to women and men.*

TRANSITIONS USED TO CONTRAST

on the other hand   *however*   *unlike*   *in contrast to*

For men, friendship means doing things together.

+ **However**, for women, friendship means talking together.

+ **Unlike** men, women think friendship means talking together.

+ **In contrast to** men, talking together is more important in female friendships.

+ **On the other hand**, American women usually identify their best friend as someone with whom they talk frequently.

All of these sentences mean:

*Friendship is **different** for men and women.*

2 *Each item below contains two sentences followed by a transition in parentheses. Write the sentences again, putting in the transition. You may need to combine some sentences. You may need to change the word order, too. For item 6, add a sentence of your own and share it with the class.*

Example

Many boys like to compete. They like to be leaders. (also)

_____Many boys like to compete. They also like to be leaders._____

1. A man might be annoyed because of the way his wife gets directions to a park or restaurant. A woman might be annoyed because of the way her husband refuses to get directions to a park or restaurant. (similarly)

   _____

2. Many women use polite forms such as "would you" and "could you." Some men don't. (in contrast to)

   _____

3. Many men like to get attention by boasting. Some women don't. (unlike)

   _____

4. Many people believe that women talk more than men. Research shows that men talk longer than women do. (however)

   _____

5. Women usually make suggestions. Men often give direct commands. (on the other hand)

   _____

6. _____

   _____

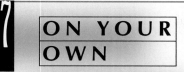

ON YOUR OWN

A. WRITING TOPICS

Choose one of the following topics. Write two or three paragraphs, using some of the vocabulary, grammar, and style you learned in this unit.

a. Are boys and girls treated differently in your home culture? Are they taught differently? Discuss similarities and differences in the ways boys and girls are treated.

b. Do you agree that men and women speak differently in your home culture? If you agree, explain the differences. Do men and women use different polite language? Do they ask for help in different ways? Do they use different word endings or beginnings? Is gossip used differently by men and women? What topics do men like to discuss with other men? What topics do women like to discuss with other women? Give examples.

c. Compare the status of men to the status of women in your home culture. How do men and women gain status?

d. Imagine a culture in which there are very few gender differences. Do you think life would be easier or more difficult? Why?

e. Some couples want to know the sex of their baby before it's born. On the other hand, some want the sex of their baby to be a surprise. What is your opinion?

B. FIELDWORK

In this unit you learned about gender differences in the United States. We can often see these cultural differences reflected in advertisements in magazines and on TV.

Step 1: Look through magazines. Find three ads that are geared for women, three ads that are geared for men, and one ad that could be for both men and women. For example, an ad for women might be for perfume, an ad for men might be for men's clothing, and an ad for both might be for a car. Fill out the form below for each ad.

1. Where magazine ad was found:
2. Product being advertised:
3. Is product for men, women, or both?
4. Do you think more men or women buy this product?

   Why?
5. Why do you think this is an ad for men or for women or for both?

6. Briefly describe the ad. Are there people in the ad? How do they look? How are they portrayed? What are their relationships to each other? What's the scene?

Step 2: In groups, compare your forms. Write a one-paragraph report on why advertisers might think about gender differences.

BREAKING THE SURFACE

I APPROACHING THE TOPIC

A. PREDICTING

Look at the photographs. Read the title of this unit. Discuss these questions with the class.

1. What is the literal (exact) meaning of the words in the title? What is the figurative (imaginative) meaning?
2. Do you know who the diver in the photograph is?
3. What is he famous for?
4. Do you know what the other picture is?
5. How could these two photographs be related?

B. SHARING INFORMATION

1 *Discuss the following questions. What do you already know about HIV (Human Immunodeficiency Virus), the virus that causes people to be sick with AIDS? What do you know about AIDS (Acquired Immune Deficiency Syndrome)? Write three things you already know.*

1. _____

2. _____

3. _____

2 *What questions do you have? Write three questions you have about HIV/AIDS.*

1. _____

2. _____

3. _____

Come back to these questions after you've finished the unit to see if your questions have been answered.

2 PREPARING TO READ

A. BACKGROUND

Below is a quiz about AIDS. Choose the best answer. Then discuss your answers with a partner.

_____ **1.** AIDS is the number one killer among people aged . . .

    a. 0–17.

    b. 18–24.

    c. 25–44.

_____ **2.** The first AIDS cases were reported in . . .

    a. 1978.

    b. 1981.

    c. 1988.

_____ **3.** The number of reported cases of AIDS in the United States from 1981 to 1995 was . . .

    a. 298,010.

    b. 501,310.

    c. 1,102,000.

_____ **4.** Since 1984, among all groups, the rate of infection has grown at a faster pace for . . .

    a. drug users.

    b. women.

    c. teenagers.

_____ **5.** By the year 2001, 58,000 children in New York State will have become orphans because . . .

    a. their single mothers died of AIDS.

    b. their single fathers died of AIDS.

    c. their single mothers died of a drug overdose.

_____ **6.** New drugs for AIDS patients . . .

    a. are helping people with AIDS be cured of AIDS.

    b. are helping people with AIDS die without pain.

    c. are helping people with AIDS live longer.

B. VOCABULARY FOR COMPREHENSION

*Read the sentences. Guess what the underlined words mean. Then decide if each statement below is true or false. Circle **T** or **F**.*

1. As the child was running down the street, he fell down and his knee started <u>bleeding</u>. When he saw the red blood, he started to cry.

    T F   The child's knee was cut, and blood was coming out.

2. I was <u>shocked</u> to hear of her death. She was so young and strong, and her life was just beginning.

    T F   I was extremely surprised.

3. The <u>trials</u> for the Olympics are almost as important as the Olympics. If you don't pass the trials, you can't go to the Olympics four weeks later.

    T F   One month before the Olympics, all the athletes must compete to see who is good enough to go to the Olympics.

4. If you drink alcohol and drive, you could <u>endanger</u> someone else's life. So, if you plan to drink, don't drive.

    T F   Someone else could be hurt or killed.

5. He found out he was <u>HIV-positive</u> ten years ago, and he died of AIDS last year.

    T F   He had the virus which causes AIDS, and it killed him.

6. The teenage mother couldn't take care of her baby, so she gave it up for <u>adoption.</u> A couple who couldn't have their own children brought the baby into their family.

    T F   The couple didn't become the baby's parents.

7. Because the woman <u>stuttered</u>, other people couldn't always understand her.

    T F   She had difficulty speaking.

8. The man was <u>beat up</u> by the robbers and left lying in the street. He had a lot of pain because of many cuts and broken bones.

    T F   The man wasn't hurt.

9. She had <u>a shot at</u> getting the job, but she didn't get it because there was one other person who had more experience.

   T   F   From the beginning, she knew she couldn't get the job.

10. Some people are afraid to dive off a three-meter <u>springboard </u>into a pool.

    T   F   People are afraid because this diving board is very high.

11. Even though he has HIV, his health hasn't changed. He is very happy that his health is <u>stable</u>.

    T   F   His health is getting worse.

READING ONE: The Last Dive

A. INTRODUCING THE TOPIC

Reading One presents some highlights from the life of Greg Louganis, an Olympic diver. It is a summary of his book, "Breaking the Surface." Read the first and second paragraphs. Write your answers to the questions below and then discuss your ideas with a partner.

Why do you think this person didn't want anyone to touch him? Why was he angry?

_____

_____

_____

The Last Dive

1   I climbed the ladder, heard my dive announced, and began the steps and jumps that would throw me into the air. Pushing off the diving board with my legs, I lifted my arms and shoulders back, and knew immediately that I was going to be close to the board and that I might hit my hands. I tried to correct myself as I turned through the air, putting my hands wide apart. Then I heard a strange sound and felt my body lose control. Moments later I realized what had happened; I had hit my head on the diving board.

2   My first feeling was embarrassment. I wanted to hide, to get out of the pool without anyone seeing me. But my next feeling was fear. Had I cut my head? Was I bleeding? Was there any blood in the pool? Swimming to the side of the pool, I noticed the shocked looks on everyone's faces. They were, of course, worried about my head; I was worried about something much more serious. A man started touching my head to see if I was bleeding. I angrily pushed him away, and everyone else who came near me. "Don't touch me!" I felt like screaming. "Get away from me!"

3   These were the trials for the 1988 Olympics in Seoul, Korea. Until this dive, I had been ahead. But now, something else was more important than my dive. I might have endangered another person's life if there had been blood in the pool. For what I knew—that no one else knew—was that I was HIV-positive.

4   According to my mother, I was a happy child. My natural parents were Samoan; that's why I have dark skin and dark eyes. They were only teenagers when I was born, so they gave me up for adoption. My new parents had adopted a girl two years before they adopted me. It was 1960. When I was only eighteen months old, I started gymnastics classes because my sister's teacher saw that I wanted to join in. Soon I was the best in the class. Later, when I was ten years old, I started trying to do gymnastics off the diving board at the pool, so my mom put me in diving classes; she was afraid I'd hurt myself. I decided I liked it as soon as I realized I was good at it.

5   School was a different story. The kids called me names because I stuttered and because of my dark skin color. I often got beat up on the way home from school. My diving gave me a way to feel good about myself when the kids at school made me feel stupid. And when I got angry because the kids beat me up and called me names, I would focus all of that anger into my diving—to be the best I could be.

6   When I was in the seventh grade, I started taking drugs. One day when I was high on drugs, I kicked my mother. Next thing I knew, the police came and arrested me. I spent three days in a prison for teenagers, sharing a room with two other kids. While I was there, my parents came to see me every day, but the other kids' parents never once came to see them. I realized that my parents really cared about me, that they were really my family, even though I was adopted. This was an important realization for me. After I left the prison, my relationship with both of my parents improved. We talked more than ever before.

7   At age sixteen, I knew I had a shot at the 1976 Olympics. At the trials, one month before the finals, I took first place on the ten-meter platform *and* on the springboard! This was surprising because I had trained mostly on the platform. In the finals, I won the silver medal for

the platform. Unfortunately, I didn't feel happy. Instead, I felt I had failed because I hadn't gotten the gold. After that, I started training with Ron O'Brien, a well-known coach of Olympic divers. Ron understood me and helped me to work harder on my diving. I soon became the leader in international diving. In the 1984 Olympics, I won two gold medals, one for the platform and one for the springboard. It was a great victory and this time I enjoyed it.

8   No one knew at that time that I was gay, except Ron and a few close friends. I kept it a secret because I was afraid—afraid of being hated if people found out. Four years later, I was preparing for the 1988 Olympics in Seoul, when I found out that the man I was living with had AIDS. I had to face the fact that I might be HIV-positive or have AIDS, too. When I finally got tested for HIV and the results came back positive, I was shocked. Was I dying? Was my shot at the '88 Olympics gone forever? What should I do? I was very confused. It was a very difficult time for me. I couldn't tell anyone because I was afraid that if people found out that I was HIV-positive, I wouldn't be able to go to the Olympics.

9   Everyone was shocked, including myself, when I hit my head on the board at the trials in Seoul. Even so, I made it into the finals, which were the following morning at 11:00. When my coach and I met to practice the next morning, he made me start with the dive I'd hit my head on. At first, I was scared, but Ron made me do it six times, and with each dive, I felt stronger. I did the rest of my dives, and we were ready.

10   During the finals, all of my dives were going well. As I entered the water on my last dive, I enjoyed for the last time the quietness underwater. Then I swam to the side of the pool to look for Ron. I was afraid to look at the scoreboard, so I watched Ron's face. Suddenly he jumped into the air, the crowd started cheering, and I knew I'd won. I won two gold medals in 1988, one for the three-meter springboard and one for the ten-meter platform. No one knew how hard it had been, except Ron and the few people who knew I was HIV-positive.

11   I quit diving professionally after the Olympics, and later did something I'd been wanting to do for a long time. I revealed that I was gay. And I also did something else I'd been wanting to do for a long time. I got a Great Dane puppy and named him Freeway. Now, I have five Great Danes and a corgi, and I really enjoy them. And I do a lot of volunteer work, like teaching people about AIDS and helping an organization called PAWS (Pets Are Wonderful Support). Since I revealed that I'm gay, I've been amazed by how people have accepted it. And even though having AIDS has forced me to stop diving, my health is stable and I'm enjoying my life.

B. READING FOR MAIN IDEAS

Fill in the chart with information about Greg Louganis so that you have a chronological record of his life. Although you may not know the exact dates for some of the events, try to find events that match the time. Use the simple present tense.

GREG LOUGANIS'S LIFE

Year	Event
1960	Greg is adopted.
1961–1962	He first shows ability in gymnastics.
1970	
1970s	He gets teased at school for having dark skin and for stuttering.
Early 1970s	
1976	
1984	
1988	He discovers he is HIV-positive. He is afraid to tell anyone because he might not be allowed to go to the Olympics.
1988	
1988	He wins two gold medals, one for the three-meter springboard and one for the ten-meter platform.
1988–Present	

C. READING FOR DETAILS

Read the details from the reading. Some of the statements have incorrect information, and some have missing information. Change the false statements so that they are true. The first one has been done for you.

1. Even though Greg's parents had always loved him very much, he never realized it.

   <u>until they came to see him every day while he was in prison.</u>

2. Although school was a painful experience for Greg, diving was also difficult and painful.

   _____

3. Greg's sister is two years younger than he is.

   _____

4. It was a surprise to everyone when he qualified for the ten-meter platform in the 1976 Olympics.

   _____

5. Greg decided to get tested for HIV because he felt sick.

   _____

6. After Greg hit his head on the springboard and got out of the pool, he screamed, "Don't touch me! Get away from me!"

   _____

7. He revealed that he was gay at the 1988 Olympics.

   _____

8. Greg started diving when he was eighteen months old.

   _____

9. In the 1984 Olympics, Greg felt he had failed when he only got the silver medal, not the gold.

   _____

10. Greg's health is getting worse.

    _____

D. READING BETWEEN THE LINES

Greg Louganis experienced many difficulties. Read the following statements about his difficulties. Go back to Reading One. Find which of the multiple choice answers below is the best answer. Sometimes more than one answer is reasonable, but one answer is better than the others.

1. One reason Greg often got beat up was because . . .
   a. he was smaller than the other kids.
   b. he wasn't as smart as the other kids.
   c. he didn't look the same as the other kids.

2. Greg kicked his mother because . . .
   a. he was a rebellious teenager.
   b. he was high on drugs.
   c. he had been beaten up by the other kids.

3. One of the things we learn about Greg as a teenager is that . . .
   a. he liked competition.
   b. he wanted to be independent.
   c. he always had to be the best.

4. Greg didn't want people to know he was gay because . . .
   a. he was afraid of not being accepted by family and friends.
   b. he was afraid people might think he was dangerous.
   c. he was afraid of losing his celebrity status.

5. When Greg found out he was HIV-positive, he kept it a secret because . . .
   a. he didn't want people to think he was gay.
   b. he didn't know if the Olympic committee would allow him to participate in the Olympics.
   c. he might endanger someone else's life.

6. When Greg hit his head in the 1988 Olympics in Seoul, Korea, his greatest worry was . . .
   a. if he would be able to win the gold medal.
   b. if another diver might get HIV/AIDS.
   c. if his coach would be angry with him.

READING TWO: PAWS—LA

A. EXPANDING THE TOPIC

1 *Read the following excerpt from a brochure about PAWS—LA.*

PAWS LA

PETS ARE WONDERFUL SUPPORT FOR PEOPLE LIVING WITH HIV/AIDS, LOS ANGELES

AGENCY OVERVIEW

1   Begun in 1989 by Nadia Sutton, PAWS/LA has grown in just six years from an organization with just two clients[1] and two volunteers to one which helps over 1,200 clients and their 1,700 pets. Understanding the importance of an animal's love to a person living with HIV/AIDS, PAWS/LA is dedicated[2] to keeping clients and the pets they love together. It is the only nonprofit[3] organization in the Los Angeles area which cares for pets whose owners are sick with this terrible illness.

2   Because the people living with HIV/AIDS are often weak and sick, these pet owners would not be able to keep, feed, and care for their pets without the help of PAWS/LA. So, volunteers for PAWS/LA walk and brush dogs, clean bird cages, and buy pet food when the people living with HIV/AIDS cannot do it themselves.

3   PAWS/LA is funded[4] by gifts of money from people who want to help. And thanks to famous volunteers such as Olympic gold medalist Greg Louganis, it has become known both nationally and internationally.

WHAT DOES PAWS/LA DO?

PAWS/LA provides:
• Pet food and supplies
• Home delivery of pet food and supplies
• Routine and emergency veterinary care
• Transportation to and from vet and grooming appointments
• Dog walking
• Litter box cleaning

• Yearly pet vaccinations
• Spay/neuter services
• Pet security deposits to people living with HIV/AIDS who have qualified for special housing with L.A. County
• Foster homes for pets when their owners are in the hospital

---

[1] *client:* a person who receives help from a professional person
[2] *dedicated:* devoted to some type of work
[3] *nonprofit:* not moneymaking
[4] *funded:* given money so it can continue

2 *Match each statement with the person you think would be most likely to make it. Then compare your answers with a partner.*

    a. Nadia Sutton   **b.** A volunteer   **c.** Greg Louganis

_____ **1.** "Friends and relatives often stop visiting them, and their pet becomes their whole world. But then they become too ill to take care of their pet. They have to give their pet away and be alone. We make sure that doesn't happen."

_____ **2.** "One day I went to visit my friend in the hospital who was sick with HIV/AIDS. He was so sad, so I asked him, 'What's the matter?' Then he told me that while he was in the hospital, his family had given away his two cats. He was so sad that he didn't want to go home! Well, I went right out, found his cats, and brought them back to him. And that was the beginning."

_____ **3.** "I love my dogs so much, and I would have a broken heart if I had to give them away, especially if I became really sick. That's why I volunteer for PAWS/LA."

B. LINKING READINGS ONE AND TWO

American nonprofit organizations often ask for money. There are many different ways to do this. One way is to have a famous person write a letter asking for money for the organization. Imagine that you are Greg Louganis and that you are writing this letter. Use what you learned from Readings One and Two and your imagination to complete the following letter.

Dear friends,

As you know, several years ago I went public on being gay. Before that, my life had not been easy. [List some of the difficulties Greg faced because of being gay and/or how you think he may have felt.] _____

_____ .

From these experiences, I realized that I wanted to help people living with AIDS. I became a volunteer for PAWS (Pets Are Wonderful Support), an organization that

_____

_____ . Founded in _____ by _____ ,

PAWS has grown from an organization with _____ to

_____ . It is the only nonprofit organization in LA which

_____ . If

not for PAWS, these people would not be able to _____ .

Volunteers for PAWS help by [list three ways in which volunteers help] _____

_____

_____

_____ . PAWS has also helped by [list at least four other ways PAWS has helped]

_____

_____

_____ . Unfortunately, there are many more

people needing PAWS than we are able to help. More money is needed to pay for the care and feeding of these pets.

PAWS is funded by donations from people who want to help—people like you. Won't you consider making a donation? Even a few dollars will help one person living with HIV/ AIDS keep the pet they love with them during their illness. Simply fill out the form on the PAWS flier and send it in. You will know that you have touched a life in a meaningful way.

Thank you for your support.

Sincerely,

Greg Louganis

Greg Louganis

5 REVIEWING LANGUAGE

A. EXPLORING LANGUAGE

Look at the vocabulary items. Below are some categories. Put each word into the category you think is best. Your answers may vary. Talk with your classmates and explain why you chose each category.

Vocabulary

arrested	endangered	a shot at	trials
beat up	HIV-positive	springboard	weak
bleeding	professionally	stable	
coach	shocked	stutter	

AIDS	Difficulties	Olympic Diving	Health

B. WORKING WITH WORDS

Read the list of analogy types. Then analyze the relationships among the vocabulary from the text. Choose the word below that best completes each analogy. Be sure that the second pair of words has a similar relationship to the first pair of words. Circle the correct answer. Then label each analogy to identify the type. The first one has been done for you.

Types of Analogies

S   Synonym: The words have the same meaning.
                    sad : depressed

A   Antonym: The words have opposite meaning.
                    sad : happy

C/E Cause/effect: One word is the result of another word.
                    smoking : heart disease

D   Degree: One word has a stronger meaning than the other.
                    nice : wonderful

U   User/tool: One word describes a person and the other word describes the tool used by the person.
                    writer : pen

N   Necessity: One word is needed for the other word to function.
                    cook : food

_S_ **1.** scared : afraid :: a shot at something : _____try_____

succeed   have   (try)

_____ **2.** afraid : terrified :: surprised : _____

worried   shocked   scared

_____ **3.** water : diving :: trials : _____

teenagers   professional   Olympics

_____ **4.** dedicated : uncommitted :: endangered : _____

safe   scared   dying

_____ 5. sick : weak :: HIV-positive : _____

angry   AIDS   confident

_____ 6. volunteer work : paid work :: nonprofit : _____

making money   client   organization

_____ 7. gymnast : parallel bars :: diver : _____

springboard   prison   scoreboard

_____ 8. homosexual : gay :: unchanging : _____

weak   stable   sick

_____ 9. failed : succeeded :: hid : _____

found out   revealed   realized

_____ 10. disliked : hated :: hit : _____

beat up   embarrassed   bled

6 SKILLS FOR EXPRESSION

A. GRAMMAR: Past Progressive and Simple Past Tense

1 *Read the following sentences and look at the underlined verbs. Notice the different forms of the verbs. What is the difference between the verb forms? Notice the boldfaced words. How are **when** and **while** different?*

◆ Greg <u>was training</u> with Ron O'Brien **when** he <u>became</u> the leader in international diving.

◆ He <u>was keeping</u> a secret **while** he <u>was preparing</u> for the Olympics.

◆ He <u>was swimming</u> to the side of the pool **when** he <u>noticed</u> the shocked looks on everyone's faces.

◆ He <u>was walking</u> his dogs **while** he <u>was listening</u> to music on his Walkman.

Past Progressive and Simple Past Tense

FOCUS ON GRAMMAR

See Past Progressive and Simple Past Tense in *Focus on Grammar, Intermediate.*

a. We use the **simple past tense** to talk about actions, states, and situations in the past that are now finished. The simple past tense of regular verbs is formed by adding **-d** or **-ed** to the base form of the verb.

- Greg **became** the leader in international diving.

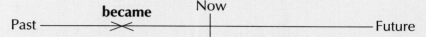

b. We use the **past progressive**, or **past continuous**, to describe an action that was in progress at a specific time in the past. The action began before the specific time and may or may not continue after the specific time. The past progressive is formed like this: **be** + **verb** + **ing**.

- Greg **was training** with Ron O'Brien.

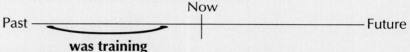

c. We use the past progressive with the simple past tense to talk about an action that was interrupted by another action. Use the simple past tense for the interrupting action. Use **when** to introduce the simple past tense action.

- Greg **was training** with Ron O'Brien **when** he **became** the leader in international diving.

d. If you put the **when-** clause first, you must put a comma at the end of the clause.

- **When** Greg became the leader in international diving, he was training with Ron O'Brien.

e. We use the past progressive with **while** to talk about two actions in progress at the same time in the past. Use the past progressive in both clauses.

- Greg **was keeping** a secret **while** he **was preparing** for the Olympics.

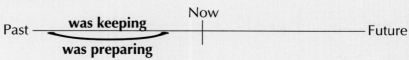

2 *Combine the two sentences in each of the following items using **when** or **while**. The first one has been done for you.*

1. Greg was swimming to the side of the pool.

   He noticed the shocked looks on people's faces.

   <u>Greg was swimming to the side of the pool when he noticed the</u>
   <u>shocked looks on people's faces.</u>

2. Greg was pushing people away.

   People were trying to touch his head.

   _____

   _____

3. Greg was living with a man who had AIDS.

   He was preparing for the 1988 Olympics.

   _____

   _____

4. Greg was preparing for the 1988 Olympics.

   He found out he was HIV-positive.

   _____

   _____

5. Greg was training with Ron O'Brien.

   He became the leader in international diving.

   _____

   _____

6. Ron was jumping into the air.

   The crowd was cheering.

   _____

   _____

3 *Now, write some sentences of your own using **when** and **while**. Think about the last time you participated in a sports event, or the last time you kept a secret. What were you doing? What were other people doing? Write three sentences with **while** and three sentences with **when**.*

1. _____

   _____

2. _____

   _____

3. _____

   _____

4. _____

   _____

5. _____

   _____

6. _____

   _____

B. STYLE: Using Narration

1 *"The Last Dive" is written as a narration, or story. Thinking about Reading One, how is a narration different from other types of writing you have done? What makes a narration, or story, effective?*

Narration

When we tell a story, we call it **narration.** There are several important parts of a good narration.

Point of view

There are two different points of view used in narration: first person (**I**) and third person (**he** or **she**). When narration is told from the point of view of **I**, we experience, or see, the story from the writer's eyes. When narration is told from the point of view of **he** or **she**, the writer is describing what someone else is experiencing.

Chronological organization

The story should have a clear beginning, middle, and end. This helps the reader understand what happened first, second, third, etc. The story has a past, present, and future. The writer must be very clear when talking about the past, the present, and the future. Transitional devices help the writer to be clear about time:

- ◆ Sequence of events: **first, second, third, then, next, after that, finally, yesterday, today, tomorrow**

- ◆ Writing about the past: **before, at that time, earlier that day, many years ago, just last week/year/month, on February 10th**

- ◆ Writing about the future: **after, later, after that, after many years**

- ◆ Two things happening at the same time: **at the same time, at that moment, meanwhile**

- ◆ Cause: **since, because**

- ◆ Writing about a result: **as a result, consequently, therefore**

A clear context

Readers should understand what, to whom, when, where, and how things happen. Look at *"The Last Dive"* as an example. In paragraph 3, the writer gives the context for paragraphs 1 and 2. He tells us the following:

- ◆ Where?   Seoul, Korea
- ◆ What?   The trials for the 1988 Olympics

If paragraph 3 were omitted, we would be very confused because we wouldn't know the **where** and **what** of paragraphs 1 and 2. Effective details also help the reader to understand clearly what is happening and to make the reading more interesting.

2 *Answer the following questions about "The Last Dive."*

1. What point of view does Greg Louganis use in his narration?

_____

2. What is the chronological organization? What is the beginning? the middle? the end?

_____

_____

_____

3. What transitional devices does Greg use in his story to show time sequence? List them below.

_____   _____   _____

_____   _____   _____

4. What is the context of Greg's narration? (Think about the whole story.)

◆ What is the story about? (What is the subject of the story?)

_____

_____

◆ To whom does the story happen?

_____

_____

◆ Where does it happen?

_____

_____

◆ When does it happen?

_____

_____

◆ How does it happen?

_____

_____

5. Find three examples of effective details Greg uses in his narration.

◆ Give one detail Greg uses in the first paragraph to describe how he hit his head on the diving board.

_____

_____

◆ Give one detail Greg uses in paragraph 6 to describe his prison experience.

_____

_____

◆ Give one detail Greg uses in paragraph 9 to describe how he prepared for the finals after hitting his head the day before.

_____

_____

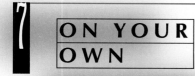

ON YOUR OWN

A. WRITING TOPICS

Choose one of the following topics. Write two or three paragraphs, using some of the vocabulary, grammar, and style you learned in this unit.

a. Write your own autobiography, describing the important events in your life. Did you have conflict with your parents? How was it resolved? Did you ever have to keep a secret during part of your life? Explain why and how you felt. What event changed your life?

b. Interview one of your classmates about his or her life. Write a biography about that person. What background information do you think you should include? What is the most interesting, exciting, emotional, or funny event in your classmate's life?

c. Write about a nonprofit organization that you (or someone you know) have been involved with. What made you (or your friend) want to help this organization? What did you (or your friend) learn from the experience?

d. Write about a personal experience you have had with someone who is gay or has AIDS, perhaps a friend. What happened? How did you feel? What did you learn from this experience?

B. FIELDWORK

Find out about organizations that help people living with HIV/AIDS. You may be able to contact a local PAWS chapter in your community.

Step 1: Contact the organization and arrange a field trip.

Step 2: Visit the organization. You may even want to volunteer to help for a day or part of a day.

Step 3: Ask these questions about the organization and add three questions of your own. Your questions can be more personal, if you wish.

a. What is the name of this organization?

b. How long has it existed?

c. Is it local, national, or international?

d. How does this organization help people with HIV/AIDS?

e. How many people does it serve?

f. How many paid staff does it have?

g. How many volunteers does it have?

h. What are some of the jobs the volunteers do?

i. Do they work with the families of people with HIV/AIDS?

j. _____

k. _____

l. _____

Step 4: Write two to three paragraphs about your feelings about the organization or about dealing with people who have HIV/AIDS.

Step 5: Share your experience by reading your paragraphs to the class.

CARS: PASSION OR PROBLEM?

SINGER

I APPROACHING THE TOPIC

A. PREDICTING

The cartoon above suggests that cars have created problems for the Earth. Work with a partner to write a caption for the cartoon. In your caption, explain the meaning of the cartoon. Then share what you have written with the class.

Example: Cars Are Eating the Earth!

B. SHARING INFORMATION

1 *Complete the chart below with your own information. Then ask two or three other students, and fill in their information.*

	DO YOU OWN A CAR?	ARE YOU INTERESTED IN CARS?	HOW OFTEN DO YOU DRIVE OR RIDE IN A CAR?
Me			
Student 1			
Student 2			
Student 3			

2 *Now look at the information in the chart and write the answers to the questions below.*

1. Who doesn't own a car? What do they use for transportation? _____

_____

_____

2. Who is the most interested in cars? For what reasons?_____

_____

_____

3. Who drives most often? _____

_____

2 PREPARING TO READ

A. BACKGROUND

Cars are a very important part of today's world. How much do you know about cars? Match the items on the right with the items on the left. Discuss your answers with the class.

_____ 1. Indianapolis 500

_____ 2. Henry Ford

_____ 3. Mille Miglia

_____ 4. pollution

_____ 5. buses and trains

_____ 6. Mercedes-Benz

_____ 7. 1903

_____ 8. Carrera Panamericana

_____ 9. Toyota

_____ 10. 2021

a. a car-related problem

b. a time when the price of a car was under $900

c. a car race in Mexico

d. an expensive car

e. a time when the world may no longer have oil

f. a car company in Japan

g. a car race in the United States

h. an early producer of cars

i. public transportation

j. a car race in Italy

B. VOCABULARY FOR COMPREHENSION

An environmentalist is someone who works to protect the environment: the air, land, and oceans of the Earth. Read the article on the next page. It describes a meeting of environmentalists who want to prepare for a future with fewer cars. Replace the underlined words and phrases with the words at the top of the page.

available   convenient   develop   engineers   fuel
industries   passion   source   technology   valuable

At a recent meeting of environmentalists, the problem of cars was discussed. Most environmentalists believe that in the future, there will be no more oil. This means that there will be no more <u>gasoline</u> for the cars that so many of us drive every day.
₁

The environmentalists agreed that cars have made our lives <u>much easier and more comfortable.</u> But they believe that it is very important for <u>the people who are working on machines</u> to try and build new ones that will not require gasoline.
₂ ₃

"We have always been good at <u>using science to create new machines</u>," said one environmentalist. "This is <u>very important</u>. Our ability <u>to build and create</u> new forms of transportation will help us face a future without gasoline."
₄ ₅ ₆

The environmentalists also discussed the importance of working with <u>businesses</u> to help them prepare for the future. "A world without gasoline means a world with fewer cars," added one man. "And this is good because it means less pollution. Maybe companies could find a way to pay extra money to workers who take buses or ride bicycles to work."
₇

Most of the people at the meeting described their <u>deep love</u> for the Earth and their desire to keep it clean. They want to power cars by using solar or electric power as <u>the place where energy comes from</u>. Both of these create less pollution than gasoline, and they will continue to be <u>usable</u> in the future.
₈ ₉ ₁₀

1. _____   5. _____   9. _____

2. _____   6. _____   10. _____

3. _____   7. _____

4. _____   8. _____

READING ONE: Cars: Passion or Problem?

A. INTRODUCING THE TOPIC

Read the first paragraph of "Cars: Passion or Problem?" Predict what the rest of the reading will be about, using the choices below. You can circle more than one answer. Then continue reading "Cars: Passion or Problem?"

1. the convenience of cars

2. the excitement of cars

3. the development of cars

4. the danger of cars

Cars: Passion or Problem?

1   For some people, the car is a convenient form of transportation. But for others, the car is an exciting hobby. Some people spend their lives collecting valuable cars. Others drive them in races, including the Mille Miglia in Italy, the Carrera Panamericana in Mexico, and the world-famous Indianapolis 500. For many people, cars are more than transportation: They are a source of passion and pleasure. Yet cars can also be a source of many problems.

2   In 1903, Henry Ford began selling the Model T car for $825. His company, Ford Motors, was the first to produce cars in large numbers. This made the car available to large numbers of people and helped them to travel long distances quickly and easily. The car has brought people much closer to places of work, study, and entertainment. Many people also work in car-related industries: fixing cars, washing cars, advertising cars, and selling car products such as stereos and cellular phones.

3   Most Americans buy a new car every five or six years. This means that one American may own a dozen cars in a lifetime. In fact, there are more cars than people in the United States. In New York City, 2.5 million cars move in and out of the city each day. In this traffic, the average speed is sometimes 8.1 miles per hour. This speed could easily be reached by riding a horse instead of driving a car. But New Yorkers continue to drive, just as people do in California, where freeways are often very crowded.

4   Some environmentalists believe that forms of public transportation such as buses and trains have not been fully developed in the United States. They try to teach others that public transportation saves fuel and helps to protect the environment. Many people are unhappy with car traffic and pollution, as well as with the use of beautiful land for building new roads. One environmentalist, Jan Lundberg, left his Mercedes-Benz in Los Angeles and moved to the forests of northern California. There he works on the *Auto-Free Times*, a newspaper that teaches people how to live without driving. Lundberg travels on foot, on bicycle, or by bus. Before he decided to live without a car, Lundberg worked for the oil companies, studying the prices of gasoline.

5   Lundberg and other environmentalists dream of turning parking lots into parks and replacing cars with bicycles, but most people around the world believe that the car is a necessary part of life in today's world. Still, there is an important question that must be answered: What kind of fuel will we use when gasoline is no longer available? Lundberg believes that by the year 2021, there will no longer be oil for gasoline makers to use. To solve this problem, car companies in Korea, Japan, Europe, and the United States are trying to develop an electric car that will not require gasoline at all.

6   The electric car is not a new idea. It had success with American women in the early 1900s. Women liked electric cars because they were quiet and did not pollute the air. Electric cars were also easier to start than gasoline-powered ones. But gasoline-powered cars were faster, and in the 1920s they became much more popular. The electric car was not used again until the 1970s, when there were serious problems with the availability of oil. Car companies began to plan for a future without gasoline. The General Motors Company had plans to develop an electric car by 1980; however, oil became available again, and this car was never produced.

7   Today there is a new interest in the electric car, which is partly related to a passion for speed and new technology. In 1977, engineer Paul MacCready designed a human-powered airplane that successfully completed a three-mile flight. A similar airplane crossed the English Channel in 1979, followed by a solar-powered airplane. In 1987, the Sunraycer, a solar-powered car, won a 2,000-mile

race in Australia. As a result of this success, the General Motors Company began new work on the development of the electric car. The Toyota Company recently decided to spend $800 million a year on the development of new car technology. Many engineers believe that the electric car will lead to other forms of technology being used for transportation.

8   Cars may change, but their importance will not. Cars are important to nearly everyone, including engineers, businesspeople, environmentalists, and even poets. Poet Curt Brown believes that cars are part of our passion for new places and new experiences. According to Brown, this "very, very comfortable flying chair" will continue to bring us travel and adventure, no matter how it changes in the future.

B. READING FOR MAIN IDEAS

1 *Look at the predictions that you made in Section 3A. Were they correct?*

2 *Number the following main ideas in the order they appear in Reading One.*

_____ **a.** Soon there will be no oil to fuel cars.

_____ **b.** Cars, whether gasoline or electric powered, will always be important.

_____ **c.** Cars can cause problems.

_____ **d.** To some people, cars are more than transportation.

_____ **e.** Some environmentalists teach people how to live without cars.

_____ **f.** People in the United States need cars to go to school, to work, and to places of entertainment.

3 *Complete the following lists with information from Reading One.*

Advantages of the Car

1. Some people enjoy _____

2. People can travel _____

3. People are closer to _____

4. Some people make money by _____

Disadvantages of the Car

1. Lots of traffic and _____

2. Cars use more fuel than _____

3. Beautiful land is replaced with _____

4. Gasoline may no longer be _____

C. READING FOR DETAILS

The outline shows how the information in the reading is organized. Read each part of the outline and cross out one detail that is not included in the reading.

I.   There are many cars in the world today.
   a. Cars were first produced in large numbers by Ford Motors.
   b. There are more cars than people in the world today.
   c. Many people have jobs that are related to cars.
   d. Two and a half million cars pass through New York City each day.

II. Cars have brought us some problems.
   a. In some areas, the air is no longer clean.
   b. Travel is sometimes slow because of traffic.
   c. Cars have made changes in the environment.
   d. Studies show that gasoline prices are increasing.

III. The car of the future may be electric.
   a. The first electric cars were faster than gasoline-powered cars.
   b. The first electric cars produced less pollution.
   c. Electric cars can be used when oil is not available.
   d. Car companies are planning to develop the electric car.

IV. Cars are very important.
   a. Many people need them in their lives.
   b. New technology is being developed because of the car.
   c. Many famous people own valuable cars.
   d. Cars bring us passion and excitement.

D. READING BETWEEN THE LINES

1 *Imagine that the following statements were made by people in a newspaper article about cars. Match the statement to the person that you think probably made it.*

a. the president of Ford Motors   **e.** a race car driver

b. a traveling businessperson   **f.** an environmentalist

c. the president of Toyota   **g.** a car collector

d. an engineer

_____ **1.** There's nothing like the feeling of speed and freedom that comes from driving a powerful car.

_____ **2.** Who cares if it's slower? The bus gives me a chance to look out the window at the trees.

_____ **3.** The freedom to travel once belonged only to the rich. Now you don't have to be rich to travel—all because of what our company did for the world.

_____ **4.** Some people spend their money on nice houses. I don't care about that. I've got a real passion for what I'm doing.

_____ **5.** You can talk about new technology all day. But until you spend your money on it, you're not really doing a thing.

_____ **6.** A lot of people don't see the connection between solar power and the electric car. But the truth is that you learn something from one and use it to develop the other.

_____ **7.** I love the idea of not knowing where I'll be next week. And all the quiet time when it's just me and the road—it gives me a chance to think.

2 *Choose two of the people listed above. Write something that these people might say. Then share what you have written with the class and have the students guess which people you have chosen.*

Example: I don't care about the danger. This kind of work has always been my dream.—race car driver

4 READING TWO: New Car Technology

A. EXPANDING THE TOPIC

1 *Look at the following diagram. What kind of new technology does it show?*

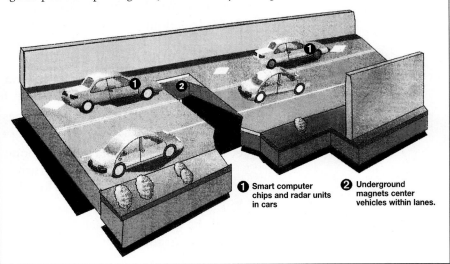

New Car Technology

A 7.16 mile stretch of carpool lane on the San Diego Freeway will be the site next year of the first test of a computerized system using magnets in the roadway to guide packs of speeding cars, with virtually no help from drivers.

1 Smart computer chips and radar units in cars

2 Underground magnets center vehicles within lanes.

Los Angeles Times

Now read the paragraph on page 145 that explains the diagram.

New Car Technology

There are plans to test new car technology on part of a freeway in San Diego, California. The cars will be driven by computers, with the help of underground magnets.[1] The magnets will keep the cars moving along the freeway. The cars will move at the same speed, with equal distance between each one. People will not have to drive. They will be able to read, work, or relax as their cars move down the freeway.

---

[1] **magnet:** an object that is able to pull other objects toward it

2 *Discuss these questions with the class.*

1. What are the main advantages of the magnetic freeway?

2. How will the magnetic freeway control traffic?

3. Some drivers may not want to drive on this freeway. Explain why.

B. LINKING READINGS ONE AND TWO

Read each statement and decide if it is true or false. Write T or F. Use information from both Readings One and Two to decide.

_____ **1.** The magnetic freeway may reduce the traffic problem.

_____ **2.** There might be more pollution because of this freeway.

_____ **3.** Electric cars will be used on the magnetic freeway.

_____ **4.** The magnetic freeway will be popular among people who have a passion for driving.

_____ **5.** Poet Curt Brown would probably enjoy the magnetic freeway.

_____ **6.** The magnetic freeway may create new car-related jobs.

REVIEWING LANGUAGE

A. EXPLORING LANGUAGE

1 *Look at the passage from Reading One. What do you notice about the underlined words?*

In 1977, engineer Paul MacCready designed a <u>human-powered</u> airplane that successfully completed a <u>three-mile</u> flight. A similar airplane crossed the English Channel in 1979, followed by a <u>solar-powered</u> airplane. In 1987, the Sunraycer, a <u>solar-powered</u> car, won a <u>2,000-mile</u> race in Australia.

Compound Adjectives

The boldfaced words are all **compound adjectives.** A compound adjective can be formed by joining a number to a noun (**three-mile**) or a noun to a past participle (**human-powered**). Another type may be formed by joining an adjective to a past participle (**solar-powered**). The two words are joined together with a hyphen (**-**). The meaning of compound adjectives comes from the meaning of the two words that have been joined. Look at the following examples:

◆ Some engineers have developed an **airplane that uses the power of humans.**

Some engineers have developed a **human-powered** airplane.

◆ One airplane completed **a flight that was three miles long.**

One airplane completed a **three-mile** flight.

PART 1

Complete each compound adjective with one of the words below.

mile   long   gasoline   six   distance   powered   related

a. _____-distance

b. sports-_____

c. short-_____

d. _____-powered

e. 26-_____

f. human-_____

g. _____-hour

PART 2

Complete the following sentences with the most appropriate compound adjective.

1. Driving a _____ car is not exercise for the body.

2. Running, on the other hand, is a _____ form of transportation.

3. Many runners enjoy _____ races known as five-kilometer, or 5K, races.

4. A _____ race is a marathon, which is much harder.

5. A marathon is a _____ race.

6. A very fast runner can complete a marathon in about three hours. But for many runners, a marathon is a _____ race.

7. During many races, people follow the runners in cars. They are available to help runners who get tired or hurt. This is an example of _____ driving.

B. WORKING WITH WORDS

A license plate is a form of car identification. It includes the name of the state in which the car is owned. In many American cities, people drive cars with personalized license plates. On these plates, the letters form a message or spell a name. Personalized license plates can tell other drivers something about the owner of the car.

1 *The following messages come from personalized license plates. Read each one and write down what you think it means. Share your answers with a partner.*

1. YBNICE _____   6. CMEFLY _____

2. BMW4ME _____   7. NOLMT _____

3. FTBOY _____   8. OBAYB _____

4. NUYRKR _____   8. 10 SNE1 _____

5. GETNBZ _____   10. MYTBIRD _____

2 *Look again at the license plate messages above. Discuss these questions in a small group.*

1. Can you find four license plate messages that are related to cars and driving? Explain their meanings.

2. Which message is related to a hobby? Explain its meaning.

3. Which two messages might belong to people who are not safe drivers? Explain their meanings.

4. Look at the other license plate messages. What can you guess about the owner of each car?

5. Why do you think so many people enjoy having personalized license plates?

3 *Use the space below to write your own personalized license plate. Then share what you have written with your classmates. Can you understand each other's messages?*

_____

_____

_____

_____

SKILLS FOR EXPRESSION

A. GRAMMAR: Future Time Clauses

1 *Read the following sentences. What do you notice about the underlined verbs?*

◆ What kind of fuel <u>will</u> we <u>use</u> when gasoline <u>is</u> no longer available?

◆ The car <u>will continue</u> to bring us travel and adventure, no matter how it <u>changes</u>.

◆ I <u>love</u> the idea of not knowing where <u>I'll drive</u> next week.

◆ When we <u>develop</u> the electric car, <u>we'll use</u> new technology.

◆ Drivers on the magnetic freeway <u>will be able</u> to relax while they <u>ride</u> in their cars.

FOCUS ON GRAMMAR

See Future Time Clauses in *Focus on Grammar, Intermediate.*

Future Time Clauses

A **clause** consists of a subject and a verb. Some sentences that describe the future have two clauses: a main clause and a time clause. One clause is in the present tense, and one is in the future tense. A time clause includes words such as **when, while, before,** and **after.** The verb in the time clause is often in the present tense. The verb in the main clause is often in the future tense. See the examples below:

                TC   MC

◆ **When** we develop the electric car, we will use new technology.

                MC   TC

◆ We will develop the electric car **before** gasoline is no longer available.
      TC

                        TC   MC

◆ **When** engineers test the magnetic freeway, they will do their work in the middle of the day.
         MC

                        TC   MC

◆ **After** we use all the oil in the world, we will have to find new sources of fuel.
         MC

                        MC   TC

◆ The drivers will race at high speeds **while** hundreds of people watch.
      TC

The time clause comes before or after the main clause. When it comes before the main clause, it is followed by a comma (,).

2 *A report was published for the people who live near a magnetic freeway. The report describes the work of the team of engineers who are building the freeway. Write the sentences by adding a present tense verb to the time clause and a future tense verb to the main clause. Add other words if necessary, using commas carefully.*

Example: check each magnet/before place it underground
<u>They will check each magnet before they place it underground.</u>

1. after place the magnets underground/count them carefully

_____

2. check the position of the magnets/while count them

_____

3. before close the underground opening/report any problems to the chief engineer

_____

4. when begin computer testing/work in two teams

_____

5. one team test the computers for speed/while the other team test them for safety

_____

6 before place the computer in the car/test it completely

_____

7. write a description of any problems/when find them

_____

8. before the freeway open/the chief engineer check it completely

_____

B. STYLE: Parallel Structure

1 *Read the following paragraph. Mark the underlined words with the correct description: **N** (noun), **V** (verb), **ADJ** (adjective), and **ADV** (adverb).*

For many people, cars are more than transportation: They are a source of <u>passion</u> and <u>pleasure</u>. The car allows people to travel long distances <u>quickly</u> and <u>easily</u>. The car has brought people much closer to places of <u>work</u>, <u>study</u>, and <u>entertainment</u>. Many people also work in car-related industries: They <u>wash</u>, <u>sell</u>, and <u>fix</u> cars. They also sell car products such as <u>stereos</u> and <u>cellular</u> <u>phones</u>. For many people, the car is <u>important</u>, <u>necessary</u>, and even <u>exciting</u>.

What do you notice about the way the above sentences are written? Which words in each sentence are the same parts of speech (nouns, verbs, adjectives, adverbs)?

Parallel Structure

Writers use **parallel structure** when they put two or three words of the same part of speech together in a series. The use of parallel structure allows writers to express several ideas in one sentence and to express these ideas clearly—and even beautifully. For example, several ideas can be expressed in one sentence.

   a. People wash cars. People fix cars. **People wash and fix cars.**

A third idea can be added:

   b. People *wash, fix, and sell cars*.

Notice that *wash, fix,* and *sell* are all present tense verbs. Now look at the following two examples:

   c. People <u>travel quickly</u> and <u>ride comfortably</u> in cars.
      V   ADV   V   ADV

In sentence (c), both phrases contain a verb and an adverb.

   d. Some people buy cars because of their <u>bright colors</u> and
      <u>comfortable seats</u>.   ADJ   N
         ADJ   N

In sentence (d), both phrases contain an adjective and a plural noun.

2 *Use parallel structure to complete the paragraph with the following words.*

passion	black	wash	valuable
slowly	give	safely	pleasure

THE CAR OF MY DREAMS

The car of my dreams is not a car at all. It is a _____ ,

_____ horse. It carries me _____ and _____

to all the places that I need to go. I take care of it every day. I _____

it and _____ it food. For me, this dream horse is a source of

_____ and _____ .

3 *Now describe the car of your dreams by completing the paragraph below. Use parallel structure.*

THE CAR OF MY DREAMS

The car of my dreams is a _____ . It is
                                              N

_____ , _____ , and
         Adj   Adj

_____ . When I need to go somewhere, it takes me
         Adj

there _____ and _____ .
              Adv   Adv

I like to _____ it and _____
              V   V

it. I especially like its _____ _____ and
                                    Adj   N

_____ _____ .
         Adj   N

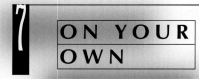

ON YOUR OWN

A. WRITING TOPICS

Choose one of the following topics. Write two or three paragraphs, using some of the vocabulary, grammar, and style that you learned in this unit.

a. Can you imagine a world without cars? What would people use for transportation? Describe what one type of transportation would look like. Explain what kind of fuel it would use and how people would travel in it.

b. How will cars change in the future? Will they be better than the cars of today? How will they help us solve the problems of traffic and pollution? Explain your idea of the car of the future.

c. In the United States, the driving age is lower than in many other parts of the world. For example, some states allow young people to drive at age fifteen. Do you think it is a good idea to allow young people to drive? Why or why not?

d. Do you or anyone you know have a passion for cars? How did this passion begin? How does this passion affect a person's life? Give examples to show how cars can be a source of passion and excitement.

e. Some people believe that cars have brought many problems into our lives—such as traffic, pollution, and accidents. Do you live in a polluted area? Have you ever had a car accident? Is traffic a part of your daily life? Explain the kinds of problems that cars have brought into your life.

B. FIELDWORK

1 *Visit a parking lot in your community. Spend fifteen to twenty minutes looking at as many cars as possible. Use the form below to record what you see.*

a. What kinds of cars (jeeps, vans, sedans, trucks, sports cars, luxury cars, etc.) do you see most often? _____

_____

b. What colors do you see most often? _____

_____

c. What is the most valuable car that you see? _____

_____

d. What is the most unusual car that you see? _____

_____

e. Did you see any cars that had personalized license plates? If so, what kind of messages did you see? _____

_____

f. Did you see any cars that were personalized in some other way? Describe what you saw. _____

_____

2 *Share your information with a small group of students. Work together to write a one-paragraph report that describes two or three of the most interesting observations made by the people in your group. For example, you may consider the type of car that seems most popular, the color that you saw most often, or the most unusual license plate. Share your report with the class.*

ALWAYS IN FASHION

COSMETIC SURGERY

◆

The

Beautiful

Woman's

Secret

◆

1 APPROACHING THE TOPIC

A. PREDICTING

Look at the newspaper ad. Take five minutes to write your answers to the following questions. Then share your answers with a partner. Do you think this type of surgery is painful? Do you know anyone who has had this kind of surgery? Do you think it is expensive? How much do you think this surgery costs?

B. SHARING INFORMATION

Complete this quiz. Read each statement, then circle the letter that best matches your opinion. Compare your answers in a small group. On which statements did you have the same opinion? On which statements did you have different opinions?

SURVEY

A = Strongly Agree B = Agree C = Disagree D = Strongly Disagree

1. Fashion is a very important part of my life.

    A   B   C   D

2. I pay attention to new clothing styles.

    A   B   C   D

3. I sometimes spend too much time and money on the way I look.

    A   B   C   D

4. I feel happier when I look good.

    A   B   C   D

5. I wish I could change the way I look.

    A   B   C   D

6. I sometimes choose my friends because of the way they look.

    A   B   C   D

7. Married people are happier if their partners are good-looking.

    A   B   C   D

8. A person will look better if he or she pays more attention to fashion.

    A   B   C   D

2 PREPARING TO READ

A. BACKGROUND

Look at the information on the timeline. Then discuss the following questions.

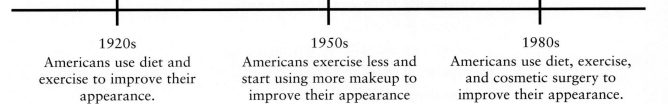

1920s	1950s	1980s
Americans use diet and exercise to improve their appearance.	Americans exercise less and start using more makeup to improve their appearance	Americans use diet, exercise, and cosmetic surgery to improve their appearance.

1. How did the American idea of beauty change in the 1950s? How did it change in the 1980s?

2. Some people use cosmetic surgery to change the way their bodies look. Do you think this is better than diet and exercise? Why or why not?

3. What kind of diet helps to improve a person's appearance? What types of exercise help people look better?

B. VOCABULARY FOR COMPREHENSION

Read the definitions. Then read the passage and fill in each blank with one of the vocabulary words. Use each word only once.

admire: to have a good opinion of someone or something

appearance: the way someone or something looks

attractive: good-looking

desire: a hope or wish

height: how tall a person is

ideal: perfect; the idea of what is perfect

modern: part of today's world

permanent: unchanging; staying the same

popular: liked by many people

slim: thin, not overweight

traditional: part of the past

weight: how heavy a person is

Fashion, or clothing style, is always changing. Fashion is never
(1) _____ . Long skirts, short skirts, pants for women,
makeup for men—these are some of the fashions that come in and out
of style. A style that is (2) _____ one year is out of style
the next.

In many countries today, people wear (3) _____ fashions
most of the time. They sometimes wear their (4) _____
clothing on special days such as holidays. For example, in Japan, people
often wear kimonos, or long silk dresses, on New Year's Day. Yet fashion is more than clothing. If you look at fashion magazines, you see
many tall, (5) _____ models. These models show that
(6) _____ and (7) _____ are an important
part of fashion. Many people (8) _____ fashion models
and wish that they could look more like them. As long as people have

the (9) _____ to be beautiful, there will be fashion.
There will always be people who follow the latest styles because they
want to look their best and be more (10) _____.These
people think that their (11) _____ is very important. They
will spend much of their time and money trying to look like the
(12) _____ man or woman.

3 READING ONE: The Search for Beauty

A. INTRODUCING THE TOPIC

The passage on pages 162-163 comes from a chapter in a book about cosmetic surgery. Read the first paragraph, then use the space below to write what you already know about fashions in the past. How have clothing styles changed? How have people's ideas about diet and exercise changed? How has the idea of beauty changed?

_____

_____

_____

_____

_____

_____

_____

_____

_____

_____

Share what you have written with the class, then continue reading "The Search for Beauty."

The Search for Beauty

1   Cosmetic surgery, also known as "plastic" surgery, is the science of changing the way a person looks by reshaping a part of the body. Cosmetic surgery also includes replacing the skin of people who have been burned and replacing the hair that some people lose as they grow older. The science of beauty has changed with time, but the desire for beauty remains the same. This chapter will discuss how fashions have changed and how these changes have led to the new modern age of cosmetic surgery.

2   People have always had the desire to look more beautiful and fashionable. Whatever their age, size, or shape, people have followed fashion in order to look more attractive. In the 1800s, for example, American women in New York began to admire the fashions of Paris. In fact, French fashions were once so popular that American dressmakers used to change their names to French ones!

3   In the 1700s, height and weight became an important part of beauty. During the time of the French Revolution, many women used to wear corsets, belts that made their waists appear much slimmer. Today we still think of the ideal person as tall and slim. But, nowadays, men or women who want to change their body shapes don't need to wear uncomfortable clothing. Instead, they can choose cosmetic surgery to reshape their bodies or to remove body fat.

4   In England in the 1500s, makeup became an important part of beauty. Some women used to paint their faces white. They thought this made them more attractive. Later, in North America, some women used to eat arsenic, a dangerous poison, to make their faces whiter. By the 1860s, American women started using makeup to make themselves more attractive. These days, women who want to look their best at all times have started using permanent makeup. Some men, especially those in show business, also use permanent makeup. The application of permanent makeup is a type of cosmetic surgery. It is much safer than using paint and arsenic, and it helps busy people save time.

5   In the 1890s, Americans discovered that bicycle riding could actually improve their appearance! They exercised in order to look and feel better. The popularity of bicycle riding even led to a change in fashion. American women began to wear shorter skirts instead of the traditional long, full ones they used to wear. By the 1920s, the beauty ideal was closely related to health, and people believed that diet and exercise were the best ways to become naturally beautiful.

6   Although diet and exercise are still popular ways of improving one's appearance, there are some parts of the body that cannot change without the help of a cosmetic surgeon. In the past, American women used to spend weeks repeating words that started with the letter "p" because they wanted to change the shape of their mouths. Today, a cosmetic surgeon can reshape the nose or lips in a few hours. Rhinoplasty, the reshaping of the nose, can greatly improve a person's appearance. People who cannot lose weight in certain areas of their bodies through diet and exercise can use liposuction, the surgical removal of body fat, to make their bodies slimmer.

7   Surprisingly, cosmetic surgery has been used for centuries in China and India. Today cosmetic surgery is used in many countries to improve the appearance of people who have been hurt in fires or in car accidents. Cosmetic surgery is also used to improve the appearance of children who are born with physical problems.

8   Is it possible that in the future everyone will look more beautiful? The answer could be yes. Cosmetic surgeons are working hard to find safer and faster ways to help people who want to change the way they look. With the help of computers, people can see their new faces before the surgery is even done. With lasers (machines that produce very strong light) cosmetic surgery can be done faster than ever before. However, like any form of surgery, cosmetic surgery can be dangerous and painful. It is also somewhat expensive for the average person. For these reasons, cosmetic surgery is not as popular today as it could be in the future. As surgeons find safer, faster, and less expensive techniques, people around the world will continue their search for beauty.

B. READING FOR MAIN IDEAS

Read the sentences that describe fashion. Then look at "The Search for Beauty" again to find sentences with similar meanings. Next to each sentence, put the number of the paragraph where you found a sentence with a similar meaning.

_____ **a.** People admired the fashions of foreign countries.

_____ **b.** Cosmetic surgery is becoming safer and faster.

_____ **c.** Women tried to change the shape of their bodies.

_____ **d.** Cosmetic surgery is not a modern science.

_____ **e.** People believed that health was an important part of beauty.

_____ **f.** Becoming beautiful may be easier in the future.

C. READING FOR DETAILS

*Read each statement and decide if it is true or false. Write **T** or **F**. If a statement is false, rewrite it to make it true.*

_____ 1. Paris was the example of fashion in the 1800s.

_____ 2. Women in France wanted to have larger waists.

_____ 3. Corsets were not comfortable.

_____ 4. Some women used paint to change the color of their faces.

_____ 5. Some men today wear permanent makeup.

_____ 6. Liposuction is often used to add body fat.

_____ 7. Cosmetic surgery is a modern science.

_____ 8. Children are not too young for cosmetic surgery.

_____ 9. Some women tried to reshape their eyes by doing exercises.

_____ 10. Some people may die during cosmetic surgery.

_____ 11. Cosmetic surgery is inexpensive.

D. READING BETWEEN THE LINES

Complete the sentences by using information from Reading One. Make a good guess based on your understanding of the information. The first one has been done for you.

1700s: During the French Revolution, women <u>wore corsets to look thinner</u> .

1800s: American women admired French fashions because _____

_____ .

1890s: People who sold bicycles _____

_____ .

1990s: Men who lose their hair _____

_____ .

2005: Cosmetic surgery will _____

_____ .

READING TWO: My Wife Wants to Look Younger

A. EXPANDING THE TOPIC

1 *Read the following diary pages written by a man whose wife decided to have a face-lift. (This is a form of cosmetic surgery that makes people look younger.)*

My Diary

Monday, April 4

Susan came home today with some surprising news. She wants to get a face-lift! She says she feels too young on the inside to look like a tired old grandma. (I thought coloring her hair made enough of a difference, but no, she wants a whole new face.) I told her that we have to meet with the doctor first. I don't want her to go into the surgery without knowing the dangers.

Tuesday, April 12

Today we sat down and talked it over with a surgeon. It's simple. The doctor cuts open the skin around the face, then lifts the skin up and pulls it back. He cuts off the extra skin and there you are, ten years younger. I watched Susan carefully while the doctor was explaining all this, and it didn't seem to bother her. I asked about the pain, and the doctor said not to expect any during surgery because of the painkiller that he'll use. It seems like doctors have all kinds of pain-killing medicine these days. After the surgery, the doctor said there might be four or five days of "discomfort." That's what he called it. I notice that he doesn't use the word "pain."

My Diary

Thursday, April 14

Susan and I stayed up late last night making our decision. We're going to do it. I told her that it doesn't matter to me at all. I love her no matter what. (Also, I don't want her to expect some fantastic change in our marriage just because she looks younger.) The doctor mentioned that, too. He said it's important not to expect too much from the surgery. Susan will look younger—that's all. It's not going to bring her instant happiness. Susan understands this. She just wants to look as young as she feels. And I wouldn't mind having a wife who looks a little younger. Who would? I just hope she won't find a younger man. Maybe I should ask the doctor if he can do anything about my bald head.

Wednesday, April 20

Susan had a medical interview today. The doctor wanted to know about her lifestyle. Susan was so glad she finally quit smoking because she could tell the doc that she's "smoke-free" and feeling good. Plus, she's more or less at her ideal weight. The doctor wanted to know how she felt about her face looking pretty bad after surgery. She told him, "Look, I've had five kids. Do you think a funny-looking face is going to scare me?" The doctor laughed and said she's in good shape physically and mentally, and I agree. Two weeks from today—that's how long we have to wait. I'm starting to wonder what she's going to look like.

My Diary

Thursday, May 5

Today's the big day. Susan's in surgery right now. She'll be in surgery for about six hours—three hours on each side of her face. It was interesting to watch the doctor take a pen and mark up her face, drawing lines for the knife to follow. Knife! Poor Susan. I hope she'll be OK.

Thursday, May 19

What a crazy time it's been! We had to put bags of frozen strawberries over her eyes and that really helped her get better. And I can't believe her face— so young and smooth. She looks fifteen years younger, and she feels great. I can see this in the way she walks and in how she spends a little more time with her makeup in the morning. The doctor says she'll look this way for about ten more years. Too bad it's not permanent. But if Susan wants to do this again, why not? I think it's worth it.

2 *Discuss these questions with the class.*

1. What kind of person do you think Susan is?

2. Do you think Susan and her husband have a good relationship? Why or why not?

3. What are some of the risks involved in cosmetic surgery? Would any of these risks stop you from having surgery?

4. Why do you think the doctor uses the word *discomfort* instead of *pain*? How will Susan avoid pain during the surgery?

3 *In the space below, write three to four sentences that might appear in Susan's diary before or after her surgery. Share your writing with a partner.*

_____

_____

_____

_____

_____

_____

B. LINKING READINGS ONE AND TWO

Look at Reading One again. Explain how cosmetic surgery can help the following people in Susan's life. In addition to cosmetic surgery, what are some other ways in which these people can improve their appearance? Work with a partner to write your answers. Then share what you have written with the class.

1. her bald husband

_____

_____

2. her older sister

_____

_____

3. her friend who cannot lose weight

_____

_____

4. her brother who wants to have a more handsome face

_____

_____

5. her neighbor who was burned in a fire

_____

_____

5 REVIEWING LANGUAGE

A. EXPLORING LANGUAGE

Read the sentences. Then rewrite each sentence, using the underlined word to express your own ideas. Use the same sentence structure. The first one has been done for you.

1. For me, the <u>ideal</u> vacation would be going to Hawaii and swimming in the ocean.

   <u>For me, the ideal vacation would be going to New York and shopping for new clothes.</u>

2. The person I <u>admire</u> most is my father because he is very intelligent.

   _____

3. If you want to see <u>popular</u> styles, look at a fashion magazine.

   _____

4. White is a <u>traditional</u> color for a bride's wedding dress.

   _____

5. I think people who smile a lot are very <u>attractive</u>.

   _____

6. <u>Slim</u> people often exercise a lot.

   _____

7. One of my <u>desires</u> is to visit Australia.

   _____

8. I think that a person's heart is more important than his <u>appearance</u>.

   _____

9. It is <u>physically</u> impossible to walk to the moon.

   _____

10. For some people, it is <u>mentally</u> difficult to remember the spelling of words.

   _____

B. WORKING WITH WORDS

Look at the following words. Then decide which ones can be used with the adjectives below from Reading One. Some words can be used more than once. The first one has been started for you.

music   color   man   body   relationship   style   personality

1. ideal: <u>man, body, relationship, personality</u>

2. modern/traditional: _____

_____

3. popular: _____

_____

4. attractive: _____

_____

5. slim: _____

_____

6. permanent: _____

_____

6 SKILLS FOR EXPRESSION

A. GRAMMAR: Describing the Past with *Used to*

1 *Read the following facts from Reading One. Underline all the sentences that include the form **used to**. What is the meaning of this form?*

In the 1700s, height and weight became an important part of beauty. During the time of the French Revolution, many women used to wear corsets, belts that made their waists appear much slimmer. . . . In England in the 1500s, makeup became an important part of beauty. Some women used to paint their faces white. They thought this made them more attractive. Later, in North America, some women used to eat arsenic, a dangerous poison, to make their faces whiter.

FOCUS ON GRAMMAR

See *Used to* in *Focus on Grammar, Intermediate.*

Describing the Past with *Used to*

Habits are actions that are repeated regularly, such as putting on makeup in the morning or getting a haircut once a month.

a. ***Used to*** can describe habits in the past.

- In the 1500s, some women **used to** paint their faces white.

- Later, others **used to** eat a dangerous poison called arsenic.

b. ***Used to*** can also describe people's attitudes.

- In the 1800s, Americans **used to** admire French style.

- During the time of the French Revolution, men **used to** admire women with small waists.

c. The negative is formed this way: ***didn't use to.***

- In the past, people **didn't use to** have liposuction to remove body fat.

- In the past, people **didn't use to** have rhinoplasty to change the shape of their noses.

2 *Look at the picture. Complete the following sentences with the correct form of **used to**.*

1. In the 1920s, Americans _____ believe that natural beauty was the best.

2. They _____ exercise in order to improve their appearance.

3. Women at that time _____ have very short, simple hairstyles.

4. They _____ spend a lot of time styling their hair or putting on makeup.

3 *Think about a fashion that you used to wear in the past. It can be clothing, shoes, or a hairstyle. Describe it in detail, using the space below.*

In the past, I used to _____

_____

_____

_____

_____

_____

_____

_____

_____

_____

I didn't use to _____ like I do today.

4 *Interview a classmate about fashions that she/he wore in the past or about fashions that people wore a long time ago in a certain part of the world. Then use the space below to write a paragraph based on information from the interview. Use the simple past tense as well as the **used to** form.*

Example

When Mari was a child, she used to wear a school uniform. Her skirt was blue, and her blouse was white. On rainy days she used to wear a blue sweater and carry a black umbrella. In the mornings her mother used to comb her hair. Her hair was very long and straight. Her mother often combed it hard. Mari didn't like this.

_____

_____

_____

_____

_____

_____

_____

B. STYLE: Giving Advice

1 *Read the following passage. Which sentences contain advice?*

If you want to keep a young-looking appearance, stay out of the sun. Too much sun will make your skin look older. If you go outside on sunny days, protect your face with a sunscreen. Protect your lips, too. Wear a good sunscreen, and cover your head with a hat. You will look younger, and you will also protect yourself from skin cancer.

Imperative Verb Form

When writers give advice, they often use the **imperative verb form**. When this form is used, the sentence begins with a verb. There is no subject. The reader understands that the subject of the sentence is *you*. Look at the following examples:

- ◆ **Stay** out of the sun.

- ◆ **Protect** your face with a sunscreen.

- ◆ **Wear** a good sunscreen.

- ◆ **Cover** your head with a hat.

The negative is formed this way:

- ◆ **Don't forget** to protect your lips.

- ◆ **Don't go** outside on a sunny day without a hat.

2 *Imagine that you are a cosmetic surgeon. You want your patients to be in good shape mentally and physically before they have surgery. Give them advice telling them what they can do to prepare for surgery.*

1. _____

   _____.

2. _____

   _____.

3. _____

   _____.

4. _____

   _____.

5. Don't _____

   _____.

6. Don't _____

   _____.

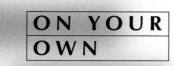

ON YOUR OWN

A. WRITING TOPICS

Choose one of the following topics. Write two or three paragraphs, using some of the vocabulary, grammar, and style that you learned in this unit.

a. Explain something that has changed in your life. Choose something that has changed as a result of moving to a new place, or something that has changed with the passing of time. What advice would you give someone who is afraid of changes?

b. Most people believe that the teenage years are a time when young people are very concerned about looking good. How did you feel about your appearance when you were a teenager? What advice would you give to teenagers who feel that they are unattractive?

c. How do you feel about growing older? What have you learned from your life? In what ways has growing older changed you? What advice would you give someone who doesn't want to get older?

d. Many people today believe that cosmetic surgery is a good way to look more like the ideal man or woman. Others believe that it is impossible to look this way, and that one's appearance is not as important as the beauty inside a person. Which opinion do you agree with more? What advice would you give to someone who is thinking about having cosmetic surgery?

B. FIELDWORK

Explore the world of fashion in your community by visiting a local department store. Go with a group of other students. First, choose one type of fashion that your group would like to examine (men's wear, women's wear, sportswear, formal wear, or something else). Next, visit that department in the store and use the following form to keep track of what you discover there. Then write a report of your findings, using some vocabulary words that you learned in this unit. Finally, exchange your report with members of another group. Discuss your reports together after you have read them.

Department: _____

Clothing items: _____

_____

_____

_____

Colors: _____

_____

Styles: _____

_____

Price range (lowest to highest): _____

Quality: _____

_____

_____

Other comments: _____

_____

_____

_____

CRIME AND PUNISHMENT

1 APPROACHING THE TOPIC

A. PREDICTING

1 Look at the photograph. Take five minutes to write your answers to the following questions. Then share your answers with a partner. What are the people doing? Where are they? What do their signs mean?

2 Work in a small group and look at the following list of words. Some of the words may be related to the photograph, and some may not. Circle the words that you think are the most closely related.

crime	opinion	justice	disagreement
agreement	murder	punishment	execution
government	protest	doctor	education

B. SHARING INFORMATION

Discuss the following questions in a small group.

1. Capital punishment means taking the life of someone who has committed[1] a crime. How many forms of capital punishment can you think of?

2. In the United States, capital punishment is allowed in some states. Do you know of any other societies in which capital punishment is allowed?

3. Why do some people believe that capital punishment is fair? Why do others think that it is unfair?

---

[1] to commit = to do

PREPARING TO READ

A. BACKGROUND

Work in a small group. Discuss punishment in two different cultures. Complete the forms below.

Culture 1: _____

Punishment for murder:	❏ Prison	❏ Execution	❏ Other:_____
Punishment for robbery:	❏ Prison	❏ Execution	❏ Other:_____
Who pays for the punishment?	❏ Taxpayers	❏ Other: _____	
What do people do in prison?	❏ Exercise	❏ Read/Write	❏ Hard physical labor
	❏ Receive physical punishment		❏ Study/Take classes
	❏ Other: _____		

Culture 2: _____

Punishment for murder:	❏ Prison	❏ Execution	❏ Other:_____
Punishment for robbery:	❏ Prison	❏ Execution	❏ Other:_____
Who pays for the punishment?	❏ Taxpayers	❏ Other: _____	
What do people do in prison?	❏ Exercise	❏ Read/Write	❏ Hard physical labor
	❏ Receive physical punishment		❏ Study/Take classes
	❏ Other: _____		

B. VOCABULARY FOR COMPREHENSION

Read the sentences and the definitions below. Then choose the best definition for the underlined words.

_____ 1. People who <u>murder</u> are very dangerous.

_____ 2. Anyone can be a <u>victim</u> of crime.

_____ 3. <u>Society</u> must find ways to stop crime.

_____ 4. There are many laws that protect <u>innocent</u> children from danger.

_____ 5. Some people who are not <u>guilty</u> have gone to prison by mistake.

_____ 6. Crime <u>destroys</u> the safety of a society.

_____ 7. <u>Execution</u> is a common form of punishment.

_____ 8. <u>Citizens</u> can work together to stop crime in their nation.

_____ 9. Some prisoners are treated with <u>cruelty</u>; they are not, for example, given food.

_____ 10. It is very difficult for people to <u>forgive</u> someone who has hurt them.

a. breaks or hurts

b. members of a nation by birth or choice

c. having done something wrong

d. pardon or excuse; let go of one's anger

e. a person who suffers as a result of wrong action

f. kill a human being

g. not having done something wrong

h. the killing of a person by a government or other power

i. unkindness or harmfulness

j. a group of people who live and work together

READING ONE:
Life in Prison Is Still Life: Why Should a Killer Live?
Why Do We Kill People to Show That Killing People Is Wrong?

A. INTRODUCING THE TOPIC

A newspaper headline is the title of a news story or an editorial. A news story gives facts about something that happened or is going to happen. An editorial gives the writer's opinion about a topic.

Look at the following editorial headlines. Write any ideas that you expect to find in each editorial. Then read the editorials on the next page.

Life in Prison Is Still Life: Why Should a Killer Live?

_____

_____

_____

_____

_____

_____

Why Do We Kill People to Show That Killing People Is Wrong?

_____

_____

_____

_____

_____

_____

Life in Prison Is Still Life: Why Should a Killer Live?

1 Murder is totally unfair. The victims of murder are gone forever. Their hopes and plans have ended. The pleasures they enjoyed in life have been destroyed. They will never see their friends again, and they will never hear the voices of parents, brothers, and sisters who cry: Why did this happen? But the murderer is still alive. Without capital punishment, murderers are allowed to enjoy life.

2 Today there are murderers in prisons all over the world. Most of them would rather spend their lives in prison than die. This is not surprising. The desire to live is normal and natural. In prison there are many small pleasures that one can enjoy every day: the feeling of warm sunshine, the taste of a hot meal, the comfort of sleep. Life in prison is not always cruel. Many prisoners are able to continue their educations, play sports, enjoy movies, and receive visits from their loved ones.

3 There is no reason why a killer, a destroyer of life, should live. Why should the tax money of citizens—including the victim's family—keep the killer alive? The only fair punishment is execution, for why should a killer live? Execution puts the killer where he belongs: away from society forever. It stops him from killing again, and it sends a strong message to others who might kill. The message is that killers will not be allowed to live.

4 Let sunshine fall on those who respect life—not on those who destroy it.

Why Do We Kill People to Show That Killing People Is Wrong?

1 There are times when killing is not done because of cruelty. Sometimes people kill because of anger, misunderstanding, or fear. All people have made mistakes because of such feelings. For society, it is a serious mistake to take the life of someone who has killed. It teaches everyone that forgiveness is impossible.

2 The government has the difficult job of deciding who is innocent and who is guilty. This job can never be done perfectly. If capital punishment is allowed, there will always be the chance that an innocent person will be executed by mistake. The U.S. government once tried to follow the example of Germany, Britain, France, and other nations that no longer execute their citizens—but now our society has accepted capital punishment again, at a high cost. We cannot imagine the pain of family members who are waiting for the government's decision to execute their loved ones—yes, no, maybe—the decision takes years. It also costs the taxpayer millions of dollars. Prison is a better form of punishment. It protects society, and it punishes criminals by taking away their freedom.

3 People can change, even people who have made terrible mistakes. Life in prison gives people the chance to change. Caryl Chessman is an example of someone who became a better person in prison. He taught other prisoners how to read, and he wrote several books. Before his execution, he wrote that he had finally learned not to hate.

4 Chessman learned this important lesson in prison. But a dead man learns nothing, and an executed person will never change. When a government kills, it is murdering hope.

B. READING FOR MAIN IDEAS

The two editorials express two different opinions about capital punishment.

Opinion A: Execution is a better form of punishment than life in prison.

Opinion B: Life in prison is a better form of punishment than execution.

In the editorials, which of the following main ideas were used to support Opinion A? Which were used to support Opinion B? Match them correctly by writing A or B. Look at Reading One again to make sure that your answers are based on information from the reading.

_____ 1. Execution may cause an innocent person to die.

_____ 2. Prisoners are able to enjoy life, and this is not fair.

_____ 3. An executed person will never commit another crime.

_____ 4. Not all people who kill are cruel.

_____ 5. A prisoner is no longer free.

_____ 6. People naturally want to live.

_____ 7. The victim's relatives must pay money to support the prisoner.

_____ 8. Prison can sometimes improve a person.

_____ 9. Execution may teach other people not to commit crimes.

_____ 10. It can be expensive to decide whether or not to execute someone.

C. READING FOR DETAILS

Match the above main ideas to the details listed below. Write the number of the main idea next to the detail. The first one has been done for you.

__4__ a. Some murders are mistakes, caused by anger or fear.

_____ b. The government spends millions of tax dollars in execution decisions.

_____ c. Most people would rather go to prison than be executed.

_____ d. Caryl Chessman learned not to hate while in prison.

_____ **e.** The message of execution is that murderers will not be allowed to live.

_____ **f.** The victim's family members must provide money for the prisoner's food and clothing.

_____ **g.** The government can make mistakes when it decides if a person is guilty or not.

_____ **h.** Prisoners have the basic pleasures of eating and sleeping.

D. READING BETWEEN THE LINES

❶ _Look back at the ideas you listed in Section 3A. Which ideas did you predict correctly? Discuss your predictions with the class._

❷ _What kind of person wrote "Life in Prison Is Still Life: Why Should a Killer Live?" Look at the following list of qualities and circle two or three that you think best describe this person._

1. believes in forgiveness

2. cares about prisoners

3. believes in fairness

4. cares about victims

5. hopes to change people

6. wants to protect society

❸ _What kind of person wrote "Why Do We Kill People to Show That Killing People Is Wrong?" Look at the following list of qualities and circle two or three that you think best describe this person._

1. cares about prison workers

2. believes freedom is important

3. cares about prisoners' families

4. wants other countries to follow the U.S.

5. believes mistakes are unusual

6. hopes that people will change

4

READING TWO: Letter to the Editor

A. EXPANDING THE TOPIC

1 *Read the following letter to the editor. In this type of letter, a person responds to an editorial that has appeared in a newspaper. The person usually agrees or disagrees with the editorial. Sometimes the person presents a new idea that is related to the editorial.*

Letter to the Editor

Dear Editor:

1   I am writing in response to your recent editorials on capital punishment. For nearly forty years, I have taught history at Coast Community College. My students have recently been discussing capital punishment. They have been trying to find reasons for their opinions. Allow me to share two true stories with your readers. They will show how difficult it is to answer the question: Is capital punishment right or wrong?

2   Back in 1920, there were two Italian immigrants named Sacco and Vanzetti. They looked "foreign," and that is why they were executed for a $16,000 robbery and murder. No one ever found the money, and no one ever found a reason for Sacco and Vanzetti to murder and rob. People who saw the crime said that the two robbers were foreign-looking. Sacco and Vanzetti looked foreign, and they did not have the money to pay for a lawyer. After seven weeks, they were found guilty. For the next six years they stayed in jail, telling everyone that they were innocent. Were they? We will never know, for both men were executed.

3   A few years later, there were two sons of rich men, named Leopold and Loeb. They killed a young boy, and then told police that they were the murderers. They were guilty, and everyone knew

it. But were they executed? No—their fathers paid for the services of Clarence Darrow, the country's best lawyer. With Mr. Darrow's help, the boys received a punishment of life in prison. They would never be executed.

4   People who believed in capital punishment were angry about the two rich boys. And people who didn't believe in capital punishment were angry about the two immigrants. But there is more to the question of capital punishment than these two sides. Innocent people can be executed, yes, but murderers can also become good people again. For example, Leopold and Loeb were busy in prison—not making trouble, but helping other prisoners learn to read and write. When Leopold was allowed to leave prison at age fifty-three, he went to Puerto Rico and spent the rest of his life working at a church hospital.

5   Was he a criminal who deserved to die? Were Sacco and Vanzetti two innocent men who deserved to live? Can we ever find a way of punishment that is fair? I don't know the answers. I only know the questions. These are the questions that people have asked in the past, and the questions that we ask ourselves today.

Very truly yours,

William Lee

2 *Discuss the following questions.*

1. What is the purpose of the letter? Does the writer express agreement or disagreement? Does the writer present a new idea?

2. Where does the writer present his main idea? Look at the letter again and underline the sentences that express the main idea.

3. Why were people angry about the Sacco and Vanzetti case? What opinion did these people have of capital punishment?

4. Why were people angry about the Leopold and Loeb case? What opinion did these people have of capital punishment?

B. LINKING READINGS ONE AND TWO

1 *Look at the editorials in Reading One again. Which one might include the two true stories as examples? Circle one of the titles below.*

1. Life in Prison Is Still Life: Why Should a Killer Live?

2. Why Do We Kill People to Show That Killing People Is Wrong?

2 *How are the two true stories related to the ideas in Reading One? Match the ideas below with one of the following:*

a. Sacco and Vanzetti

b. Leopold and Loeb

_____ 1. Many prisoners may be able to continue their educations.

_____ 2. There will always be the chance that an innocent person will be executed.

_____ 3. People change, sometimes for the better.

_____ 4. An executed person will never change.

5 REVIEWING LANGUAGE

A. EXPLORING VOCABULARY

1 *Some nouns refer to ideas or feelings. They refer to things that cannot be seen or touched such as love and peace. These nouns are called* **abstract nouns.** *Look at the following list of nouns, and mark the abstract nouns with A.*

_____ 1. forgiveness   _____ 5. punishment

_____ 2. friends   _____ 6. prison

_____ 3. misunderstanding   _____ 7. food

_____ 4. anger   _____ 8. citizen

2 *When writers use abstract nouns, they often use examples to help the reader understand more clearly what they mean. Read the examples below, then match them to the appropriate abstract noun.*

_____ 1. cutting off the hand of a person who steals

_____ 2. a judge deciding that someone is a murderer

_____ 3. deciding not to stay angry when someone has hurt you

_____ 4. making all citizens pay taxes to the government

_____ 5. choosing to do something that breaks the law

_____ 6. hurting an animal for no reason

_____ 7. carrying the passport of a particular country

_____ 8. relatives, friends, and neighbors

_____ 9. a judge deciding that someone did not rob a bank

_____ 10. people moving from Mexico to California

a. forgiveness

b. cruelty

c. innocence

d. society

e. citizenship

f. guilt

g. immigration

h. punishment

i. fairness

j. crime

❸ *Complete the passage with one of the following words. The first one has been done for you.*

citizenship   cruelty   fairness   forgiveness   guilt

innocence   immigration   punishment   society

   The story of Leopold and Loeb is one of (1) ___guilt___ , not
(2) _____ . Everyone knew that they had murdered a young
boy for no reason. But their parents were able to pay for the services of
a good lawyer because they belonged to the highest level of
(3) _____ . The lawyer succeeded in stopping the execution
of Leopold and Loeb. Some citizens were angry about this because of
the (4) _____ of the murder. For the family of the murdered
boy, this was not an example of (5) _____ . Instead, it was
an example of the fact that wealthy people are often able to avoid
(6) _____ . No one knows if the relatives of the murdered
boy were ever able to offer their (7) _____ to Leopold and
Loeb. But it is a well-known fact that Leopold and Loeb were sorry for
what they had done. Leopold spent the rest of his life caring for sick
people after his (8) _____ to another land. Loeb showed
good (9) _____ by following all the rules in prison and
helping other prisoners learn to read.

B. WORKING WITH WORDS

*In editorial writing, writers choose their words carefully. They want to
present their opinions as strongly as possible because they want the
reader to agree with them. Look at the following pairs of sentences.
Complete sentence b by choosing the best word to replace the
underlined word in sentence a. How does the meaning change
when you use a different word? Circle the appropriate responses.*

1. a. A government is wrong when it <u>kills</u> its citizens.

   b. A government is wrong when it _____ its citizens.
                                 (punishes, executes)

   New meaning: Weaker   Stronger   Neither

2. a. Why should we keep a <u>murderer</u> alive?

   b. Why should we keep a _____ alive?
   (criminal, victim)

   New meaning: Weaker   Stronger   Neither

3. a. Life in prison is not always <u>bad</u>.

   b. Life in prison is not always _____ .
   (fair, cruel)

   New meaning: Weaker   Stronger   Neither

4. a. Prisoners hope to receive visits from <u>the people who care about them</u>.

   b. Prisoners hope to receive visits from their _____ .
   (loved ones, relatives)

   New meaning: Weaker   Stronger   Neither

5. a. Men and women who follow the laws of their country are usually good <u>people</u>.

   b. Men and women who follow the laws of their country are usually good _____ .
   (adults, citizens)

   New meaning: Weaker   Stronger   Neither

6. a <u>Immigrants</u> are sometimes the victims of crime.

   b. _____ are sometimes the victims of crime.
   (Strangers, Foreigners)

   New meaning: Weaker   Stronger   Neither

7. a. The government decides whether people are <u>wrong</u>.

   b. The government decides whether people are _____ .
   (guilty, innocent)

   New meaning: Weaker   Stronger   Neither

8. a. Many people fear prison because they believe it will <u>hurt</u> their future.

   b. Many people fear prison because they believe it will _____ their future.
   (change, destroy)

   New meaning: Weaker   Stronger   Neither

SKILLS FOR EXPRESSION

A. GRAMMAR: Contrast—Present Perfect and Present Perfect Progressive

1 *Read the following passage from the "Letter to the Editor" in Reading Two. Look at the underlined verb forms. Discuss the questions with the class.*

Letter to the Editor

I am writing in response to your recent editorials on capital punishment. For nearly forty years, I <u>have taught</u> history at Coast Community College. My students <u>have recently been discussing</u> capital punishment. It is very difficult to answer the question: Is capital punishment right or wrong? Can we ever find a way of punishment that is fair? I don't know the answers. I only know the questions. These are the questions that people <u>have asked</u> in the past, and the questions that we ask ourselves today.

1. What tense are the verbs?

2. When do we use the present perfect?

3. When do we use the present perfect progressive?

Present Perfect and Present Perfect Progressive

FOCUS ON GRAMMAR

See Contrast: Present Perfect and Present Perfect Progressive in *Focus on Grammar, Intermediate.*

a. Use the **present perfect** form to indicate that an action is completed.

  ◆ I **have taught** this history class several times. (Completed action)

Use the **present perfect progressive** to show that an action that began in the past is still continuing.

  ◆ I **have been teaching** history for nearly forty years. (Continuous action)

b. The present perfect emphasizes the permanence of an action or situation.

  ◆ Crime **has become** a serious problem. (Permanent situation)

The present perfect progressive indicates that an action or situation may be temporary.

  ◆ Some people **have been protesting** the use of capital punishment. (Temporary situation)

c. Use the present perfect and the present perfect progressive with the time expressions *for* and *since*. Both forms are sometimes used with adverbs such as *always* and *recently*.

  ◆ Crime **has always been** a part of society.

  ◆ Some people **have been** criminals **since** they were young.

  ◆ Different governments **have been executing** criminals **for many years.**

  ◆ **Recently,** some states in the U.S. **have been using** capital punishment again.

d. Nonaction verbs, such as *be*, and verbs that refer to mental states or emotions (*believe, wish, trust*) are not used in the present progressive.

  ◆ For most prisoners, life in prison **has been** difficult.

  ◆ Many prisoners **have wished** that they could be free.

  ◆ Most family members **have believed** in the innocence of their loved ones in prison.

2 *Read this passage, which describes the life of a prisoner.*
Add the present perfect or the present perfect progressive forms
of the verbs in parentheses.

Wayne Paulson _____ in prison since 1992. For
1. (be)

three years he _____ for the government's decision
2. (wait)

whether or not to execute him. Lately, he _____ letters
3. (write)

because he wants to make sure that his loved ones understand that he is

innocent. He _____ very lonely in prison. Only a few
4. (be)

people _____ him. But one person _____
5. (visit)   6. (come)

to see him nearly every day—his mother. She will visit him as long as he

remains in prison, because she _____ that her son is not
7. (always/believe)

guilty. Wayne's mother _____ everyone that her
8. (tell)

son is a good citizen. She will continue to do this as often as she can

because she _____ her son since the day he was born.
9. (love)

B. STYLE: Sentence Variety

1 *Look at the following sentences from Reading One. How are they different from each other? Which sentence is the longest? Which one is the shortest? Which sentences consist of two ideas that are joined together?*

1. Most of them would rather spend their lives in prison than die.

2. This is not surprising.

3. The desire to live is normal and natural.

4. Prison is a better form of punishment.

5. It protects society, and it punishes criminals by taking away their freedom.

Writers use a variety of sentence types to make their writing more interesting to read. Sentences can be short, long, or medium in length. Simple sentences consist of only one subject and one verb. Compound sentences consist of two or more subjects and two or more verbs. Look at the following examples:

$$S \qquad\qquad V$$
The <u>victims of murder</u> <u>are</u> gone forever. (Simple)

$$S \qquad V \qquad\qquad\qquad\qquad S \qquad\qquad V$$
<u>They</u> <u>will never see</u> their friends again, and <u>they</u> <u>will never hear</u> the voices of their parents, brothers, and sisters. (Compound)

The second example contains two simple sentences that are joined together with **and**. The first sentence is followed by a comma. The second sentence begins with the conjunction **and**. Two sentences can also be joined together with the conjunctions **but**, **so**, and **or**.

2 *Change the following simple sentences into compound sentences. Add a comma (,) after the first sentence and then use a conjunction (**and, but, so, or**) to join the second sentence to the first one.*

Example: **a.** Wayne Paulson lives in prison.   **b.** He rarely sees his friends.
  <u>Wayne Paulson lives in prison, so he rarely sees his friends.</u>

1. a. He is lonely.   **b.** He is also worried about his future.

_____

2. a. He says that he is innocent.   **b.** Few people believe him.

_____

3. a. His mother doesn't want him to feel lonely.   **b.** She has visited him almost every day.

_____

4. a. Wayne Paulson may be executed.   **b.** He may spend his life in prison.

_____

3 *Read the following letter written by Wayne Paulson to a friend. Rewrite the sentences so that the letter contains a variety of sentence lengths: long, short, and medium. You may combine short sentences by using a conjunction, or you may shorten long sentences by removing a conjunction and writing two simple sentences. Make at least three changes.*

Dear Tom,

It has been two years since I've seen you. I miss you and all my friends a lot. I wish I could see you soon. I know you might think that I'm guilty. Maybe you don't want to see me anymore. But I will always be your good friend Wayne. Please remember all the good times we had. Please remember how you have always trusted me. I hope that you will come see me soon. I hope that you will keep me in your thoughts.

Your friend,

Wayne

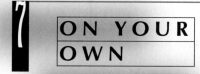

7 ON YOUR OWN

A. WRITING TOPICS

Choose one of the following topics. Write two or three paragraphs, using some of the vocabulary, grammar, and style that you learned in this unit.

a. Write a letter to Wayne Paulson. Explain what you have learned about the question of capital punishment. Give him some advice about what he might do in prison to make the best possible use of his time.

b. Imagine that in your local area, capital punishment has been illegal for several years. Now the government plans to begin using it again. Write a letter to the editor of your local newspaper expressing your opinion of capital punishment.

c. Discuss whether or not children are punished by society in your home culture. If so, what kinds of punishment are given? For example, are children sent to prison? Do you think it is a good idea to punish children?

d. At times, people who visit foreign countries have trouble with the law. When they are punished, they sometimes receive stronger punishments than they would in their home countries. Do you believe that certain countries give punishments that are too strong?

B. FIELDWORK

1 *Find out how people in your local area learn about crimes that happen in their towns or cities. Look in some of the places listed below for information about local crimes.*

    a. your local newspaper

    b. your school newspaper

    c. mail sent to private homes

    d. pictures of criminals at the post office or police station

    e. missing children announcements on milk cartons

    f. reports from the police station

    g. [other] _____

2 *Use the form below to organize the information that you find.*

    a. What type of information did you find? Where did you find it?

        Type   Place Found

        _____   _____

        _____   _____

        _____   _____

        _____   _____

    b. Do you think that people in your local area need more information about crimes that are happening around them?

        Yes ❑   No ❑   Maybe ❑

        What are some possible ways that this information could be given to them?

        _____

        _____

        _____

3 *Work in a small group to discuss the information that you found. Write a one-paragraph report in which you explain what you learned from this fieldwork.*

FINDING A SPOUSE

1 APPROACHING THE TOPIC

A. PREDICTING

Read the following joke. Then discuss the questions with the class.

> Marriage has three rings: an engagement ring, a wedding ring, and suffering.

1. Do you understand the joke's meaning? Do you think it's funny?
2. Do you agree that suffering is a part of marriage? Why or why not?
3. In your home culture, do men or women wear wedding or engagement rings? In what other ways do they show that they are married or engaged?

B. SHARING INFORMATION

People choose marriage partners for various reasons. Which of the following reasons for choosing a marriage partner is important to you? Mark each one from 1 to 5 (1= not important; 5= very important). Then discuss your choices with a partner.

_____ **a.** ability to have children

_____ **b.** partner's age

_____ **c.** parents' choice

_____ **d.** religion

_____ **e.** love

PREPARING TO READ

A. BACKGROUND

Test your knowledge of marriage customs around the world. Read the sentences below and choose the culture that you think practices the custom described in each sentence. Write the letter that corresponds to the culture next to each sentence. There may be more than one correct choice.

a. Arab   **b.** German   **c.** Native American   **d.** Vietnamese

e. Chinese   **f.** Mexican   **g.** North American

_____ **1.** Young women often read magazines for wedding advice.

_____ **2.** Girls are allowed to choose their favorite boy for a husband.

_____ **3.** Young women used to invite men to visit them at night by leaving their windows open.

_____ **4.** Men and women usually decide to get married without any advice from their parents.

_____ **5.** Parents usually choose a marriage partner for their children.

_____ **6.** A man may have more than one wife.

_____ **7.** Marriage partners sometimes do not know each other before their wedding.

B. VOCABULARY FOR COMPREHENSION

Complete the crossword puzzle: Read the clues below, then choose the correct word to write in each space.

background	fertility	produce	romantic
characteristics	leadership	raise	spouse
community	pregnancy		

Across

1. Past experience, including family life and education
2. To make or create
3. To take care of children as they grow from babies to adults
4. Features or qualities that belong to an animal, person, or object
5. A group of people who live and work together

Down

1. Related to strong feelings of love between a man and a woman
2. The physical condition during which a baby develops inside a woman's body
3. A husband or a wife
4. The ability to have children
5. The ability to direct other people

READING ONE: Finding a Spouse

A. INTRODUCING THE TOPIC

The following article appeared in a journal for students of anthropology (the study of how human beings live together in communities). Read the first paragraph of the article. Then answer the questions.

What about you? If you are married, how did you find your spouse? If you are single, what do you think is the best way for you to find a spouse?

Share your answers with a partner, then read the rest of the article.

Finding a Spouse

1   All human beings are born into families—and families begin with the joining together of a man and a woman in marriage. All societies have their own form of marriage. The ideas that we have about marriage are part of our cultural background; they are part of our basic beliefs about right and wrong. As we study marriage, we find that different cultures have solved the problem of finding a spouse in different ways. Finding a marriage partner has never been easy for people, no matter when or where they have lived.

2   In traditional Chinese culture, marriage decisions were made by parents for their children. Parents who wanted to find a spouse for their son or daughter asked a matchmaker to find someone with the right characteristics, including age and educational background. According to the Chinese way of thinking, it would be a serious mistake to allow two young people to follow their romantic feelings and choose their own partners. The all-important decision of marriage was made by older family members, who understood that the goal of marriage was to produce healthy sons. In traditional Chinese society, sons were important because they would take positions of leadership in the family and keep the family name alive.

3   As part of our cultural background, beliefs about marriage can be as different as the cultures of the world. While the traditional

Chinese did not believe that young people should be free to choose their own marriage partners, the Hopi, a native people of North America, had a very different idea about freedom. The Hopi allowed boys to leave their parents' home at age thirteen to live in a *kiva,* a special home for young males. Here they enjoyed the freedom to go out alone at night and secretly visit young girls. Most boys tried to leave the girl's home before daylight, but a girl's parents usually did not get angry about the night visits. They allowed the visits to continue if they thought the boy was someone who would make a good marriage partner. After a few months of receiving visits, most girls became pregnant. At this time they could choose their favorite boy for a husband.

4   The Hopi culture is not the only one that allowed young people to visit each other at night. Some Bavarian people of southern Germany once had a "windowing" custom that took place when young women left their windows open at night so that young men could enter their bedrooms. When a woman became pregnant, the man usually asked her to marry him. But women who did not get pregnant after windowing were often unable to find a husband. This was because fertility was a very important requirement for women in this culture, and the windowing custom allowed them to prove their fertility to others in the community. Some people are surprised when they learn of this custom because they expect the people of southern Germany to follow the rules of the Catholic religion, which teach that it is wrong for unmarried women to become pregnant. But the windowing custom is only one example of the surprising views of marriage that are found around the world, even among people whose religious beliefs require more common marriage practices.

5   One view of marriage that surprises most of us today was held by John Noyes, a religious man who started the Oneida Community in the state of New York in 1831. Noyes decided that group marriage was the best way for men and women to live together. In this form of marriage, men and women changed partners frequently. They were expected to love all members of the community equally. Children belonged to all members of the community, and all the adults worked hard to support themselves and shared everything they had. Members of the Oneida Community lived together for a while without any serious problems; however, this way of life ended when John Noyes left in 1876. Without his leadership and special way of thinking, members of the community quickly returned to the traditional marriage of one woman and one man.

6   A more famous example of a different style of marriage is found among the early Mormons. The group's first leader, Joseph Smith, believed that a man should be allowed to have several wives. As the Mormon Church grew, many of the men followed Smith's teaching and married a number of wives. The Mormons believed that it was a woman's duty to marry at a young age and raise as many children as possible. For example, in 1854, one Mormon leader became a father nine times in one week when nine of his wives all had babies. Today the Mormon Church teaches that marriage should be a partnership of one man and one woman who will be together not only during this life but also forever.

7   Today there are some men who might agree with the custom of allowing a man to have as many wives as he chooses. Many young lovers today dream of the freedom of the Hopi, and some of us wish that a matchmaker would help us find the perfect mate. Finding a spouse with whom we can spend a lifetime has always been an important concern. Despite all the different ways of finding a marriage partner, one idea is the same throughout the world: Marriage is a basic and important part of human life.

B. READING FOR MAIN IDEAS

The following sentences describe cultural beliefs. Match each belief to the culture in which it exists

a. Hopi   **b.** Bavarian   **c.** Oneida Community   **d.** Chinese   **e.** Mormon

_____ **1.** Young people are not capable of making the right marriage choices for themselves.

_____ **2.** Getting pregnant shows that you will be a good wife.

_____ **3.** Women should get married as early in their lives as possible.

_____ **4.** A girl should be free to choose her own husband.

_____ **5.** It is better for society if people are not limited to one marriage partner.

C. READING FOR DETAILS

Write a brief answer to each of the following questions. Then check your answers with a partner.

1. Who helped Chinese parents choose a spouse for their sons or daughters? How did this person help?

_____

2. What was the Chinese idea of a successful marriage?

_____

3. Why did Hopi parents sometimes stop night visits?

_____

4. What do people in some Catholic countries believe about unmarried women?

_____

5. What did John Noyes believe about marriage?

_____

6. How has the Mormon idea of marriage changed?

_____

D. READING BETWEEN THE LINES

Read about the following problems. For each problem, identify the culture in which the problem could be taking place. Describe the cultural belief that may be related to the problem.

Example

A girl cannot marry the boy she loves because another girl has already chosen him for a husband.

Culture: <u>Hopi</u>

Cultural Belief: <u>It's a good idea to let girls choose who they want for a</u>
<u>husband.</u>

1. A husband is upset because his wife has given birth to another daughter.

   Culture: _____

   Cultural Belief: _____

2. A woman is very jealous of her best friend because she is pregnant.

   Culture: _____

   Cultural Belief: _____

3. A man doesn't want his wife to love another man, but he is afraid to tell her how he feels.

   Culture: _____

   Cultural Belief: _____

4. Two sisters are worried that they will have to separate because they won't be able to marry the same man.

Culture: _____

Cultural Belief: _____

5. Two young lovers wish they could spend their lives together, but they cannot.

Culture: _____

Cultural Belief: _____

6. A girl and her parents are fighting because they don't want the boy she loves to see her.

Culture: _____

Cultural Belief: _____

READING TWO: What's Wrong with Tradition?

A. EXPANDING THE TOPIC

The following letter appeared in the student newspaper of an American university. It was written by an international student who believes strongly in his country's traditional way of choosing spouses.

Letter to the Editor

Dear Editor:

1   I am a twenty-seven-year-old student from Vietnam. My purpose in coming here is to get a business degree. I am very grateful to have the chance to get an education in a country of such great business leadership. However, I am tired of the questions that people ask me about my personal life. American students seem to think that their way of dating romantically before marriage is the only way, but I disagree. Let me give you an example from my own life.

2   My parents have been married for thirty-five years. Their marriage has all the characteristics of a happy one: deep friendship, love, and trust. They have six children, and I am the second son.

Because of their help, I am able to study in the United States. They have always worked hard to raise their children in the right way. When I finish my degree, I will go back to my country and help them.

3   American people are always surprised when I tell them that my parents met for the first time on their wedding day. Americans can't believe that such a marriage could be happy, but I have seen my parents with my own eyes. They love each other faithfully, and they are proud of the children that their marriage has produced. They learned to love each other slowly, as time passed. I believe they share a true and everlasting love.

4   When people ask, "Are you looking for a girl-friend?" I tell them no. For me, studying comes first. When I go back to my country and start working, my parents will help me find a good wife. She will be someone with a good family background, someone I can trust. Good apples come from good trees. If I marry a good apple, we can make a beautiful, growing tree together. No divorce. No AIDS. No broken heart.

5   I want a peaceful, happy life just like my parents have. Why can't Americans understand this?

Paul Nguyen

Use the space below to write your response to Paul Nguyen's letter. Then share what you have written with the class.

Dear Paul Nguyen,

I am writing in response to your letter that appeared in the student news-

paper. I would like to share my opinion with you. I believe that _____

_____ . This is because _____

_____ . I also have a question for you. _____

_____ ? In my opinion,

_____ . Thank you

for allowing me to share my thoughts.

Sincerely,

_____

B. LINKING READINGS ONE AND TWO

1 *Discuss these questions in a small group.*

1. Paul Nguyen explains that his parents met on their wedding day. Who do you think made the decision for this couple to get married?

2. Consider your own parents. When did they meet? How did they meet? Who made the decision for them to get married?

2 *Think about marriage in the various cultures that you have learned about in Readings One and Two. Are men and women both free to choose their marriage partners, or is this decision made for them by someone else? Look at the graph below. Give each of the following cultures a number according to where you think it belongs on the graph. Discuss your choices in a small group.*

Marriage Decision   Marriage Decision
Is Made Freely   Is Not Made Freely

| 10 | 9 | 8 | 7 | 6 | 5 | 4 | 3 | 2 | 1 |

_____ **a.** Hopi   _____ **d.** Vietnamese

_____ **b.** Bavarian   _____ **e.** Mormon

_____ **c.** Chinese   _____ **f.** Oneida Community

5 REVIEWING LANGUAGE

A. EXPLORING LANGUAGE

Courtship takes place when a man and a woman get to know each other before marriage. In some cultures, they spend time together alone. In other cultures, they spend time together with friends and relatives. During this time, a couple may decide whether or not to marry.

*Read the sentences below and decide if they are related to courtship (**C**), a wedding ceremony (**W**), or married life (**M**). Write the appropriate letter next to each sentence. Then put the sentences in a time order that makes sense. Write a number next to each sentence. The first one has been done for you.*

_____ **a.** Members of the community are invited to watch the couple promise to love each other for a lifetime.

_____ **b.** The man gives the woman flowers to show his romantic feelings for the first time.

_____ **c.** The husband and wife disagree about the best way to raise their two sons.

_____ **d.** Friends and relatives throw rice at the couple to make a wish for their fertility.

_____ **e.** The husband and wife hope that their marriage will produce healthy children.

_C-1_ **f.** A man and a woman are attracted to each other because of such characteristics as good looks, intelligence, and kindness.

_____ **g.** Important words are spoken by a person in a position of leadership.

_____ **h.** The woman happily tells her mother that she is pregnant.

_____ **i.** The man decides that the woman will be an excellent spouse.

_____ **j.** Little by little, each partner learns more about the other's background.

B. WORKING WITH WORDS

*Look at the following pairs of words. Decide whether they are similar in meaning (**synonyms**) or opposite in meaning (**antonyms**). Some pairs are neither similar nor opposite; decide whether or not they are related in meaning. Write the appropriate letter next to each pair. Then discuss your answers with a partner.*

S: synonym   **R:** related

A: antonym   **NR:** not related

_____ 1. characteristics
features

_____ 2. spouse
husband

_____ 3. marriage
divorce

_____ 4. background
family

_____ 5. single
couple

_____ 6. leadership
group

_____ 7. equal
religious

_____ 8. raise
produce

_____ 9. romantic
faithful

_____ 10. everlasting
forever

_____ 11. brokenhearted
proud

_____ 12. infertility
pregnancy

_____ 13. tough
suffering

_____ 14. engagement
courtship

6 SKILLS FOR EXPRESSION

A. GRAMMAR: Articles—Definite and Indefinite

1 *Look at the following passage from "Finding a Spouse." Underline the indefinite article a. Circle the definite article the. How are these articles different in meaning?*

The Hopi culture is not the only one that allowed young people to visit each other at night. In southern Germany, the windowing custom took place when young women left their windows open so that young men could enter their bedrooms. When a woman became pregnant, the man usually asked her to marry him.

Articles: Definite and Indefinite

FOCUS ON GRAMMAR

See Articles: Definite and Indefinite in *Focus on Grammar, Intermediate.*

a. Use the definite article *the* when you have a particular person, place, or thing in mind.

- ◆ **The** Hopi culture is not the only one that allowed young people to visit each other at night.

- ◆ In southern Germany, **the** windowing custom took place when young women left their windows open at night.

b. Use the indefinite article *a* when you do not have a particular person, place, or thing in mind. Use the indefinite article *an* before words that begin with vowel sounds.

- ◆ **An** older woman is sometimes **a** matchmaker.

- ◆ When **a** boy turned thirteen, **the** Hopi culture allowed him to leave home.

Notice that in the above example, the indefinite article *a* is used for *boy* because the writer does not have a particular boy in mind. The definite article *the* is used for *Hopi culture* because, in this case, the writer is referring to a particular culture.

c. When you refer to something more than once, use the indefinite article *a* the first time you mention a person, place, or thing. Then use the definite article *the* after the first mention.

- ◆ In most cultures, it is important for **a** wife to have children. **The** wife must raise her children well.

- ◆ In the United States, **a** man usually asks **a** woman to be his wife. When **the** man asks this question, he often gives **the** woman **a** diamond engagement ring.

2 *Complete the paragraphs below with the indefinite article **a(n)** or the definite article **the**.*

PLANNING A WEDDING

(1) _____ American bride often looks in (2) _____ bridal magazine for advice about planning (3) _____ wedding. Every bride has her own idea of (4) _____ perfect wedding. For most brides, this includes flowers, music, and (5) _____ delicious wedding cake. Most magazines also provide information about planning (6) _____ romantic trip. Some brides dream of going to (7) _____ warm beach, while others wish to travel to (8) _____ distant country. Bridal magazines also give advice about following traditional American wedding customs. For example, (9) _____ bride will sometimes give (10) _____ piece of wedding cake to her friends. Each friend takes (11) _____ piece of cake home and places it underneath her pillow. According to tradition, if (12) _____ woman does this, she will dream of her future husband at night. (13) _____ woman will see his face in her dreams.

B. STYLE: Using Related Word Forms for Cohesion

1 *In a well-written text, the ideas are cohesive; that is, they fit together clearly. The word for this clear fitting together of ideas is* **cohesion.** *Look at the following paragraphs. Which one, a or b, has more cohesion? Why?*

a. Many women do not feel very romantic when they are pregnant. They feel unhappy, fat, and unattractive. This can sometimes be a rather difficult time in their marriage. Yet they look forward to the birth of their child.

b. Many women do not feel very romantic when they are pregnant. Their feelings of romance disappear during pregnancy because they feel fat and unattractive. Pregnancy is sometimes a difficult time in their marriage. Yet married women look forward to the birth of their child.

Writers use related word forms to gain more **cohesion** in their writing. In paragraph **b**, the ideas fit together clearly because the writer uses such related word forms as *romantic* and *romance, pregnant* and *pregnancy,* and *marriage* and *married.* The use of related word forms helps the writer move smoothly from one idea to the next. The writer is able to keep the reader's focus on the main idea without repeating the same exact words again and again. Look at the following example:

Other pregnant women believe that they are quite **beautiful** during pregnancy. Their **beauty** comes from the joy of becoming a mother. There is a light in their eyes, and their skin shines **beautifully.**

2 *Read the pairs of sentences below. Then add the word in parentheses to each sentence, changing the form of the word as needed.*

Example: (education) Chinese parents believe that _education_ is very important. As a result, they are interested in the _educational_ background of a person who wants to marry their son or daughter.

1. (religion)   According to the Mormon _____ , a man could have several wives. Mormon families were usually quite large because of this _____ belief.

2. (spouse)   Choosing a _____ is a difficult decision. People have different ideas about the best _____ characteristics.

3. (courtship)   In some cultures, young people are not free to _____ each other by themselves. Their _____ is controlled by an older person.

4. (person)   In some European countries, marriage is a _____ decision. It is usually made by each _____ , without the control of older family members.

5. (engagement)   If a woman agrees to marry a man, she becomes _____ to him. She will often receive a ring as a symbol of _____ .

6. (ceremony)   A wedding _____ is a special event that most people enjoy. Some of the _____ songs are quite famous.

7. (leadership)   John Noyes was the _____ of the Oneida Community. The members of this community practice group marriage as a result of his _____ .

8. (traditional)　The United States has a _____ of using white as the main color of weddings. Therefore most _____ wedding dresses are white.

9. (faithful)　If spouses are _____ , they will love each other for a lifetime. Their _____ will produce a happy family life.

❸ *Use the space below to write your own sentences. Choose three pairs of words from the above exercise.*

1. _____

_____

2. _____

_____

3. _____

_____

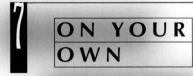

ON YOUR OWN

A. WRITING TOPICS

Choose one of the following topics. Write two or three paragraphs, using some of the grammar, vocabulary, and style that you learned in this unit.

a. What are the characteristics of a good spouse? Give examples to support your opinion.

b. What are the characteristics of a happy marriage? Do these characteristics change with the passing of time? Or do they remain the same?

c. Do you believe that using a matchmaker can be a good way to find a spouse? Why or why not?

d. Describe a marriage or courtship custom with which you are familiar. Is this custom related to religion? Explain.

B. FIELDWORK

*Read the personal advertisement section of a newspaper or look for personal advertisements on the Internet. Before you read the ads, make sure that you understand the abbreviations that are used. For example, **DWF** means "divorced white female," and **SBM** means "single black male." Most personal advertisement sections have an abbreviation key that explains the meanings. Find three or four ads placed by people who are describing the kind of partner that they desire to marry. Use the following chart to organize the information that you find.*

	CHARACTERISTICS OF AD WRITER	CHARACTERISTICS OF DESIRED PARTNER
Ad 1		
Ad 2		
Ad 3		
Ad 4		

Next, work in a small group to compare the information that you found. Which ad writer do you think is most likely to find a marriage partner? Why? Which one is least likely to find one? Why? Write one paragraph to explain your opinion.

ANSWER KEY

UNIT 1 ◆
THE WORLD OF ADVERTISING

2A. BACKGROUND
1. F   2. T   3. F   4. F

2B. VOCABULARY FOR COMPREHENSION
1. succeed	6. campaign
2. fail	7. message
3. market	8. global
4. firm	9. convince
5. goal	10. competition

3B. READING FOR MAIN IDEAS
1 Sentence 3: When advertisers write an ad, their goal is to make people want to buy the product. Sentence 4: Laws about advertising are different all over the world.

2 1. Jacko is an Australian football player who appeared in the battery ads. His failure in the U.S. campaign shows that advertisers need to change their campaigns when they advertise in different countries.

2. The translation could be wrong. A wrong translation may send the wrong message.

3. The global advertiser must pay attention to different communication styles as well as different laws and customs.

4. A company should do this because people in different countries have different likes and dislikes.

3C. READING FOR DETAILS
1. a	3. b	5. c	7. d
2. c	4. b	6. d	8. b

3D. READING BETWEEN THE LINES
(Suggested answers.)

1. No. People in Canada may have different tastes than people from Mexico. The company should also plan a new campaign for Canada.

2. No. The translation could be wrong, so it's a better idea to rewrite the ads in Japanese.

3. Maybe. The company might find success by advertising on TV. But it is impossible that this type of advertising is not allowed in those countries.

4. Yes. It's very important to sell different products in different parts of the world. The company's product will be right for the Saudi Arabian market.

4B. LINKING READINGS ONE AND TWO
Answers will vary.

5A. EXPLORING LANGUAGE
2. b	4. b	6. d	8. a
3. c	5. c	7. c	

5B. WORKING WITH WORDS
1. c	3. f	5. d	7. h
2. e	4. g	6. a	8. b

6A. GRAMMAR: Simple Present Tense and Present Aggressive
1 1. are having
   are planning
   are discussing
   are writing down
2. present progressive
3. want
   hope
   care
   (simple present)

2 1. make   4. is increasing
2. are losing   5. serve
3. believe   6. consider

6B. STYLE: Paragraph Development
1 1. The main ideas are found in the first and last sentences.
2. The examples are found in the second and third sentences.
3. There are three examples.

2 1. D3   3. D2   5. CS
2. D1   4. TS

UNIT 2 ◆ TELECOMMUTING: GOING HOME TO WORK

2B. VOCABULARY FOR COMPREHENSION

1. relaxed
2. stressed
3. person who commutes to work
4. can't bend
5. problem
6. joined
7. be afraid of
8. over the phone
9. find something you lost
10. participate in society

3B. READING FOR MAIN IDEAS

1. T   3. F   5. T
2. T   4. T   6. F

3C. READING FOR DETAILS

	Paragraph
1. c	
2. c	3
3. b	3
4. a	3
5. c	4
6. c	6
7. a	7
8. b	8
9. c	9
10. a	10

3D. READING BETWEEN THE LINES

2 1. a   3. c   5. a   7. c
   2. c   4. b   6. b   8. a, b, c

4A. EXPANDING THE TOPIC

1 1. administrative
   2. assistant
   3. company
   4. experience
   5. individual
   6. insurance
   7. manager
   8. minimum
   9. necessary
   10. with
   11. word processing
   12. years

2 1. a. mid 30s
      b. typing and word processing
      c. Y
   2. a. minimum two years experience
      b. a media company
      c. N

   3. a. a motivated person
      b. minimum two years experience
      c. N
   4. a. monthly
      b. five
      c. Y
   5. a. long-distance phone services
      b. none
      c. Y
   6. a. word processing, with experience with tables and charts
      b. days, nights or weekends
      c. Y

4B. LINKING READINGS ONE AND TWO

Answers will vary.

5A. EXPLORING LANGUAGE

1. d   3. a   5. b
2. c   4. f   6. e

5B. WORKING WITH WORDS

2. indoor air
3. lonely
4. modem
5. past
6. relocate
7. computer message
8. alone
9. desocializing of society
10. e-mail

6A. GRAMMAR: Modals and Related Verbs That Show Ability

2 1. will be able to
   2. be able to
   3. can/am able to
   4. can't/am not able to
   5. can/am able to
   6. can/am able to
   7. couldn't
   8. can
   9. be able to
   10. be able to

6B. STYLE: Letter Writing

3 date = March 13
salutation = Dear Barbara
body = Thank you for . . . Write soon!
close = Love
signature = Helene

UNIT 3 ◆ A MIRACLE CURE?

2B. VOCABULARY FOR COMPREHENSION

1. a	**6.** a
2. b	**7.** c
3. b	**8.** a
4. c	**9.** b
5. c	**10.** a

3B. READING FOR MAIN IDEAS

1. a	Paragraph 7
2. c	3
3. b	5
4. b	8
5. a	6
6. c	4

3C. READING FOR DETAILS

1. g, 3	**5.** b, 6
2. f, 5	**6.** e, 2
3. d, 2	**7.** a, 6
4. c, 4	

3D. READING BETWEEN THE LINES

Answers will vary. Following are suggestions.

2. Did the person selling the product say that the product is good for many different illnesses?

3. Did s/he offer a money-back guarantee?

4. If the treatment requires you to go to a clinic, is this clinic in another country?

5. Did the person invite you to read a testimonial?

6. Did the person promise a quick, exciting cure?

7. Did the person say that the product is made in a secret way or with something secret that can only be purchased through this company?

4A. EXPANDING THE TOPIC

2 Answers may vary. Following are suggestions.

1. Reading Two is an advertisement for a cancer clinic named "The Organic Health Center."

2. He claims that he learned the causes and cure of cancer as he traveled around the world. In fact, however, he has no real medical training.

3. A special diet consisting of herbs combined with healthy foods.

4B. LINKING READINGS ONE AND TWO

2. Their products are good for many illnesses.

2. "My health center specializes in curing cancer and other diseases."
Paragraph 1
"Program C: For all other diseases"
Paragraph 5

3. They offer money-back guarantees.

3. "I provide a money-back guaranteed if the program fails."
Paragraph 7

4. They invite you to read testimonials.

4. "...I have testimonials for you to read."
Paragraph 6

5. They promise quick, exciting cures.

5. "After one to six months, you will be cured of cancer."
Paragraph 4

6. The product/treatment is made in a secret way and is only available from them.

6. "This cure is available only at the Organic Health Center."
Paragraph 2

7. They say that doctors and/or the rest of the medical community are against them.

7. "That's why doctors will tell you not to trust me."
Paragraph 3

2 Answers will vary. The important task for the students is to be able to give good reasons based on the readings for their answers. Those who practice Western medicine would probably choose c and h as the "real treatments."

5A. EXPLORING LANGUAGE

1. offered	6. frauds
2. arthritis	7. founder
3. unproven	8. specializes
4. guarantee	9. victim
5. discovery	10. harmless

5B. WORKING WITH WORDS

Answers will vary.

6A. GRAMMAR: Adjectives—Superlative

2
1. the worst	6. the fastest
2. the most educated	7. the most dedicated
3. the most intelligent	8. the most helpful
4. the easiest	9. the healthiest
5. the best	

6B. STYLE: Summary Writing

2
1. SD2	5. SD3
2. SD5	6. SD6
3. TS	7. SD1
4. SD4	

6B

3 Many people are using quacks instead of doctors. <u>Unfortunately</u>, these people often don't realize how dangerous it is to use a quack. It is dangerous because the product usually doesn't work. <u>As a result</u>, the patient can be getting worse during the treatment. People often go to quacks because they want an easy solution for their problem and because they are afraid. Quacks understand this. <u>So</u> they sell products for illnesses that have no cure, and people who are afraid of dying will pay any price for them. It can be difficult to know if someone is a quack, but there are ways. <u>Quacks also</u> use similar techniques for selling their products. If you are concerned about buying something from a quack, there are people and organizations that can help you.

UNIT 4 ◆ THE METAMORPHOSIS

2B. VOCABULARY FOR COMPREHENSION

2
1. f	4. a	7. b	10. e
2. h	5. d	8. i	11. g
3. j	6. k	9. c	

3B. READING FOR MAIN IDEAS

1. Gregor has become/is an insect.
2. His family is shocked/frightened.
3. Only his sister takes care of him, but eventually she loses interest.
4. His family wants to get rid of him.
5. He feels helpless.
6. He dies in his room as he thinks of his family.

3C. READING FOR DETAILS

2. This worked better, but he still couldn't move enough to get out of bed.
3. Gregor panicked and said, "No, no; I will come out immediately."
4. The manager began to back out of the room slowly, and Gregor realized he couldn't let him leave.
5. He slid under the couch and slept there until morning.
6. The next morning, Gregor's sister looked in and was surprised to see that he hadn't eaten a thing.
7. The first few didn't hurt him, but then one pierced his body, and he felt terrible pain.
8. His sister also began to care less and less about feeding him and cleaning his room.
9. We must find a way to get rid of this thing.
10. He lay there in the dark and couldn't move.

3D. READING BETWEEN THE LINES

Answers will vary.

4B. LINKING READINGS ONE AND TWO

Answers will vary.

5A. EXPLORING VOCABULARY

Answers will vary, except for number 2.

1, c	3, b
2, a	4, d

5B. WORKING WITH WORDS

2 b. fell   g. stuck
c. wept   h. forgot
d. awoke   i. thought
e. slept   j. found
f. felt   k. took

6A. GRAMMAR: Infinitives of Purpose

1 a. to support
b. to ask
c. to get out
They answer the question <u>why</u>.

2 2. f   5. c
3. g   6. b
4. a   7. e

3 2. Gregor was locked in his room to keep him there.

3. His father grabbed a walking stick and newspaper to beat him.

4. Grete went into Gregor's room every day to feed him.

5. Gregor followed Grete into the dining room to help her.

6. Gregor came out of his room to listen to the music.

7. His family took a train ride to celebrate his death.

6B. STYLE: Paraphrasing

1 2. to get up   6. amazed
3. quickly come out   7. cut into him
4. knew   8. taking care of him
5. sofa   9. to remove
            10. darkness

2 Answers will vary.

3 Answers will vary.

UNIT 5 ◆
SPEAKING OF GENDER. . .

2B. VOCABULARY FOR COMPREHENSION

2. a   5. c   8. a   11. b
3. b   6. a   9. a
4. c   7. b   10. c

3A. INTRODUCING THE TOPIC

1. They told their relatives and friends that the baby would be a girl.

2. The friends and relatives sent gifts, including pink dresses and dolls.

3B. READING FOR MAIN IDEAS

2. T
3. T
4. F: Gender differences . . . when they **play**
5. F: Differences in language . . . are **different** in all cultures
6. F: **Boys** gain status . . .
7. T
8. F: **Women** usually talk more . . . than **men** do
9. T
10. T

3C. READING FOR DETAILS

2. a   Paragraph 1   7. a   9
3. b   2   8. c   10
4. b   4   9. c   10
5. a   5   10. b   11
6. c   7

3D. READING BETWEEN THE LINES

1. a   Paragraph 1   5. b   3
2. c   1 & 2   6. a   6
3. b   2   7. a   7
4. c   5 & 2   8. a, b   9, 10, 11

4B. LINKING READINGS ONE AND TWO
Answers will vary.

5A. EXPLORING LANGUAGE

1. F   4. F   7. F   10. F
2. M   5. F   8. M   11. F
3. M   6. M   9. M   12. F

5B. WORKING WITH WORDS

1. gender   6. influence
2. compete   7. reflects
3. masculine   8. emphasizes, proves
4. feminine   9. status
5. fair   10. prove, emphasize

6A. GRAMMAR: Using Modals for Requests

2 1. Could you speak louder?

2. Could you repeat that one more time?

3. Can you tell me what you mean?

4. Could you say that again?

5. Would you mind speaking more slowly?

3 Answers may vary.

6B. STYLE: Comparing and Contrasting

2 1. A man might be annoyed because of the way his wife gets directions to a park or restaurant. <u>Similarly</u>, a woman might be annoyed because of the way her husband refuses to get directions to a park or restaurant.

2. <u>In contrast to men</u>, many women use polite forms such as "would you" and "could you."

3. <u>Unlike</u> women, many men like to get atttention by boasting.

4. Many people believe that women talk more than men. <u>However</u>, research shows that men talk longer than women do.

5. Women usually make suggestions. <u>On the other hand</u>, men often give direct commands.

UNIT 6 ◆
BREAKING THE SURFACE

2A. BACKGROUND

1. c   3. b   5. a
2. b   4. b   6. c

2B. VOCABULARY FOR COMPREHENSION

1. T   4. T   7. T   10. T
2. T   5. T   8. F   11. F
3. T   6. F   9. F

3B. READING FOR MAIN IDEAS

Answers may vary.

1970	He starts taking diving lessons.
Early 1970s	He takes drugs, kicks his mother, is arrested, spends 3 days in prison, and realizes how much his parents care for him.
1976	He wins the silver medal for the platform.
1984	He wins two gold medals—one for the 3-meter springboard and one for the 10-meter platform.
1988	He hits his head on the diving board during the trials for the 1988 Olympics and worries that he might have endangered someone's life.
1988-Present	He quits diving professionally, reveals he is gay, gets five Great Danes and a corgi, volunteers for PAWS, and is experiencing stable health.

3C. READING FOR DETAILS

Answers may vary.

2. While school was a painful experience for Greg, diving was not difficult and painful.

3. Greg's sister is two years older than he is.

4. It was a surprise to everyone when he qualified for the three-meter springboard in the 1976 Olympics.

5. Greg decided to get tested for HIV because his roommate had AIDS.

6. After Greg hit his head on the springboard and got out of the pool, he wanted to scream "Don't touch me! Get away from me!"

7. He revealed that he was gay after the 1988 Olympics.

8. Greg started gymnastics when he was eighteen months old.

9. In the 1976 Olympics, Greg felt he had failed when he only got the silver medal, not the gold.

10. Greg's health is stable.

3D. READING BETWEEN THE LINES

1. c   3. c   5. b
2. b   4. a   6. b

4A. EXPANDING THE TOPIC

2 1. b, 2. a 3., c

4B. LINKING READINGS ONE AND TWO

1. Answers may vary.

2. is dedicated to keeping people with HIV/AIDS and the pets they love together.

3. 1989

4. Nadia Sutton

5. only two clients and two volunteers

6. one which helps over 1,200 clients and their 1,700 pets.

7. helps people with HIV/AIDS who own pets.

8. keep, feed, and care for their pets.

9. Answers will vary.

10. Answers will vary.

5A. EXPLORING LANGUAGE
Answers will vary.

5B. WORKING WITH WORDS

2. D   shocked

3. N   Olympics

4. A   safe

5. C/E   AIDS

6. A   making money

7. U   springboard

8. S   stable

9. A   revealed

10. D   beat up

6A. GRAMMAR: Past Progressive and Simple Past Tense

2 2. Greg was pushing people away while they were trying to touch his head.

3. Greg was living with a man who had AIDS while he was preparing for the 1988 Olympics.

4. When Greg found out he was HIV-positive, he was preparing for the 1988 Olympics.

5. When Greg became the leader in international diving, he was training with Ron O'Brien.

6. Ron was jumping into the air while the crowd was cheering.

6B. STYLE: Using Narration

2 Answers may vary.

1. "I", first person

2. Beginning—his background and childhood
Middle—his diving career
End—his retirement from diving
He starts the story with one of his dives during the trials for the 1988 Olympics, which is actually the middle of the story, for greater drama.

3. then, next, later, after, at that time, before

4. What?   Diving and HIV/AIDS
   To whom?   Greg Louganis
   Where?   Most of the story happens in the United States, but some parts happen in other countries, such as Seoul, Korea
   When?   The story covers Greg's life from birth to approximately 34.
   How?   Greg becomes a diver as a result of doing gymnastics off of a diving board. His mother put him in diving classes because she was afraid he'd hurt himself. He catches HIV/AIDS from his roommate perhaps.

5. **a.** "I lifted my arms and shoulders back, and knew immediately that I was going to be close to the board and that I might hit my hands."

   b. "I spent three days in a prison for teenagers, sharing a room with two other kids."

   c. "When my coach and I met to practice the next morning, he made me start with the dive I'd hit my head on."

UNIT 7 ◆
CARS: PASSION OR PROBLEM?

2A. BACKGROUND

1. g	3. j	5. i	7. b	9. f
2. h	4. a	6. d	8. c	10. e

2B. VOCABULARY FOR COMPREHENSION

1. fuel	6. develop
2. convenient	7. industries
3. engineers	8. passion
4. technology	9. source
5. valuable	10. available

3B. READING FOR MAIN IDEAS

2 a. 5   d. 1
   b. 6   e. 4
   c. 3   f. 2

3 Advantages of the Car
   1. Some people enjoy collecting and racing cars.
   2. People can travel long distances quickly and easily.
   3. People are closer to work, school, and entertainment.
   4. Some people make money by working in car-related industries.

   Disadvantages of the Car
   1. Lots of traffic and pollution
   2. Cars use more fuel than buses and trains
   3. Beautiful land is replaced with roads
   4. Gasoline may no longer be available

3C. READING FOR DETAILS

I. b   III. a
II. d   IV. c

3D. READING BETWEEN THE LINES

1. e   5. c
2. f   6. d
3. a   7. b
4. g

4B. LINKING READINGS ONE AND TWO

(Suggested answers.)
1. T   3. F   5. T
2. F   4. F   6. T

5A. EXPLORING LANGUAGE

Part 1. Word Formation
   a. long-distance   e. 26-mile
   b. sports-related   f. human-powered
   c. short-distance   g. six-hour
   d. gasoline-powered

Part 2. Sentence Completion
   1. gasoline-powered   5. 26-mile
   2. human-powered   6. six-hour
   3. short-distance   7. sports-related
   4. long-distance

5B. WORKING WITH WORDS

1 1. Why Be Nice   6. See Me Fly
   2. BMW For Me   7. No Limit
   3. Fat Boy   8. Oh Baby
   4. New Yorker   9. Tennis Anyone
   5. Getting Bs   10. My T-Bird

6A. GRAMMAR: Future Time Clauses

2 1. After they place the magnets underground, they will count them carefully.
   2. They will check the position of the magnets while they count them.
   3. Before they close the underground opening, they will report any problems to the chief engineer.
   4. When they begin computer testing, they will work in two teams.
   5. One team will test the computers for speed while the other team tests them for safety.
   6. Before they place the computer in the car, they will test it completely.
   7. They will write a description of any problems when they find them.
   8. Before the freeway opens, the chief engineer will check it completely.

6B. STYLE: Parallel Structure

1
ADV	ADJ
quickly	important
easily	necessary
	exciting

N	V
passion	wash
pleasure	sell
work	fix
study	
entertainment	
stereos	
cellular phones	

2 The car of my dreams is not a car at all. It is <u>valuable</u>, <u>white</u> horse. It carries me slowly and <u>safely</u> to all the places that I need to go. I take care of it every day. I <u>wash</u> it and <u>give</u> it food. For me, this dream horse is a source of <u>passion</u> and <u>pleasure</u>.

Note: Adjectives of value (valuable) come before adjectives of color (white).

UNIT 8 ◆ ALWAYS IN FASHION

2B. VOCABULARY FOR COMPREHENSION

1. permanent	5. slim	9. desire
2. popular	6. height	10. attractive
3. modern	7. weight	11. appearance
4. traditional	8. admire	12. ideal

3B. READING FOR MAIN IDEAS

a. 2	c. 3	e. 5
b. 8	d. 7	f. 8

3C. READING FOR DETAILS

1. T	4. T	7. F	10. T
2. F	5. T	8. T	11. F
3. T	6. F	9. F	

3D. READING BETWEEN THE LINES

(Answers may vary.)

1800s: American women admired French fashion because they made women look attractive.

1890s: People who sold bicycles made a lot of money.

1990s: Men who lose their hair have it replaced.

2005: Cosmetic surgery will be safer and faster.

4B. LINKING READINGS ONE AND TWO

(Suggested answers.)
1. He can have his hair replaced.
2. She can have a face lift, or she can use makeup.
3. She can have liposuction, or she can diet and exercise.
4. He can have rhinoplasty, or he can use permanent makeup.
5. She can use cosmetic surgery to improve her appearance.

5A. EXPLORING LANGUAGE

Answers will vary.

5B. WORKING WITH WORDS

(Answers may vary.)
2. Modern/Traditional: music, man, relationship, style
3. Popular: music, man, style
4. Attractive: color, man, body, style
5. Slim: man, body
6. Permanent: color, relationship

6A. GRAMMAR: Describing the Past with *Used To*

2 1. used to believe   3. used to have
     2. used to exercise   4. didn't used to spend

6B. STYLE: Giving Advice

1. The first, third, fourth, and fifth sentences give advice.

UNIT 9 ◆ CRIME AND PUNISHMENT

2B. VOCABULARY FOR COMPREHENSION

1. f	3. j	5. c	7. h	9. i
2. e	4. g	6. a	8. b	10. d

3B. READING FOR MAIN IDEAS

1. B	3. A	5. B	7. A	9. A
2. A	4. B	6. A	8. B	10. B

3C. READING FOR DETAILS

b. 10	d. 8	f. 7	h. 2
c. 6	e. 9	g. 1	

3D. READING BETWEEN THE LINES

2 Answers may vary. Suggested answers: 3, 4, and 6

3 Answers may vary. Suggested answers: 2, 3, and 6

4A. EXPANDING THE TOPIC

2 1. The purpose of the letter is to present a new idea: the question of capital punishment is a very difficult one to answer.

   2. The main idea is expressed in the last sentence of the first paragraph. Another important idea is expressed in the second line of the last paragraph: "Can we ever find a way of punishment that is fair?"

   3. People were angry because there was no clear proof that Sacco and Vanzetti were guilty. People who react this way usually disagree with capital punishment.

   4. People were angry because the boys were guilty, yet they were not executed. People who react this way usually agree with capital punishment.

4B. LINKING READINGS ONE AND TWO

1 2

2 1. b   3. b
2. a   4. a

5A. EXPLORING VOCABULARY

1 1, 3, 4, and 5

2 1. h   3. a   5. j   7. e   9. e
2. f   4. h   6. b   8. d   10. g

3 2. innocence   7. forgiveness
3. society   8. immigration
4. cruelty   9. citizenship
5. fairness
6. punishment

5B. WORKING WITH WORDS

(Answers may vary.)

1. executes (weaker)   5. citizens (neither)
2. criminal (neither)   6. Foreigners (neither)
3. cruel (stronger)   7. guilty (stronger)
4. loved ones (stronger)   8. destroy (stronger)

6A. GRAMMAR: Contrast—Present Perfect and Present Perfect Progressive

2 1. has been   6. has been coming
2. has been waiting   7. has always believed
3. has been writing   8. has been telling
4. has been   9. has loved
5. have visited

6B. STYLE: Sentence Variety

1 The sentences differ in length. Sentence (5) is the longest. Sentence (2) is the shortest. Sentences (3) and (5) consist of two ideas that are joined together.

2 (Suggested answers.)
1. He is lonely, and he is also worried about his future.
2. He says that he is innocent, but few people believe him.
3. His mother doesn't want him to feel lonely, so she has visited him almost every day.
4. Wayne Paulson may be executed, or he may spend his life in prison.

3 One suggested response:

It has been two years since I've seen you, and I miss you and all my friends a lot. I wish I could see you soon, but I know that you might think I'm guilty. Maybe you don't want to see me any more. But I will always be your good friend Wayne. Please remember all the good times we had, and please remember how you have always trusted me. I hope that you will come see me soon. Keep me in your thoughts.

UNIT 10 ◆ FINDING A SPOUSE

2A. BACKGROUND

(Suggested answers.)
1. g   5. e
2. c   6. a
3. b   7. d
4. g

2B. VOCABULARY FOR COMPREHENSION

ACROSS	DOWN
1. background	1. romantic
2. produce	2. pregnant
3. raise	3. spouse
4. characteristics	4. fertility
5. community	5. leadership

3B. READING FOR MAIN IDEAS

1. d   4. a
2. b   5. c
3. e

3C. READING FOR DETAILS

1. A matchmaker helped them. A matchmaker's job was to find a marriage partner with the right characteristics.
2. A successful marriage was one that produced sons.
3. They stopped night visits if they thought a boy would not be a good husband.
4. It's wrong for unmarried women to get pregnant.
5. He disagreed with traditional marriage because he believed that group marriage was the best way for men and women to live together.

6. Today the Mormons believe that marriage is a partnership of one man and one woman who will be together forever.

3D. READING BETWEEN THE LINES

(Suggested answers.)

1. Culture: Chinese; Cultural Belief: the purpose of marriage is to produce sons
2. Culture: Bavarian; Cultural Belief: women should be fertile
3. Culture: Oneida Community; Cultural Belief: all community members should love each other equally
4. Culture: Mormon; Cultural Belief: A man should be allowed to choose several wives.
5. Culture: Chinese; Cultural Belief: Young people should not be free to choose their own marriage partners.
6. Culture: Hopi; Cultural Belief: Parents can decide if a boy will be a good husband or not.

4B. LINKING READINGS ONE AND TWO

2 (Suggested answers.)

   a. 9 (spouse chosen by girl; parents usually agree)
   b. 9 (man chooses a woman following her pregnancy)
   c. 1 (controlled by parents)
   d. 1 (controlled by parents)
   e. 3 (controlled by men)
   f. 3 (controlled by the teachings of the community)

5A. EXPLORING LANGUAGE

(The time order in the first few items related to courtship may vary.)

a. W-5	f. C-1
b. C-3	g. W-6
c. M-10	h. M-9
d. W-7	i. C-4
e. M-8	j. C-2

5B. WORKING WITH WORDS

1. S	5. A	9. NR	13. R
2. R	6. R	10. S	14. R
3. A	7. NR	11. NR	
4. R	8. R	12. A	

6A. GRAMMAR: Articles—Definite and Indefinite

2
1. an	4. the	7. a	10. a	13. the
2. a	5. a	8. a	11. the	
3. a	6. a	9. a	12. a	

6B. STYLE: Using Related Word Forms for Cohesion

1. religion; religious
2. spouse; spousal
3. court; courtship
4. personal; person
5. engaged; engagement
6. ceremony; ceremonial
7. leader; leadership
8. tradition; traditional
9. faithful; faithfulness

20
44
62
58